MW00975099

From A Cook To Professional Chef

From A Cook To Professional Chef

The Culinarian Vol. I

Benny Diaz

iUniverse, Inc.

New York   Bloomington   Shanghai

From A Cook To Professional Chef
The Culinarian Vol. I

Copyright © 2008 by Benny Diaz

iUniverse books may be ordered through booksellers or by contacting:

iUniverse
1663 Liberty Drive
Bloomington, IN 47403
www.iuniverse.com
1-800-Authors (1-800-288-4677)

Because of the dynamic nature of the Internet, any Web addresses or links contained in this book may have changed since publication and may no longer be valid.

The views expressed in this work are solely those of the author and do not necessarily reflect the views of the publisher, and the publisher hereby disclaims any responsibility for them.

ISBN: 978-0-595-48380-8 (pbk)
ISBN: 978-0-595-71795-8 (cloth)
ISBN: 978-0-595-60471-5 (ebk)

Printed in the United States of America

CONTENTS

Winemakers

Sanitation and Food Handling

Terminology
- 41°F-135°F—Temperature Danger Zone
- Spores—Spores are created by bacteria in order to survive their environment, either above boiling point of water or below freezing level
- IPM—Innergrated Past Management
- 15 Second—The recommended amount of time food must be held at cooking temperature
- FDA—Food and Drug Administration
- 32°F—Freezing temperature of water
- PHF—Potentially Hazardous Foods
- CCP—Critical Control Points
- Air Gap—the space between the facet and the sink used to prevent the backflow of bacteria
- Quats—the level at which ammonia is graded
- PCO—Pest Control Operator
- Cold Paddle—Use to chill food quickly, usually a known reacting container filled with water then frozen
- Ph 4.6 to 7.5—Optimum level for certain bacterial growth
- Fifo—First in First Out

The Unsafe Food Handler
food handlers can contaminate food in numerous ways, from when they prepare it to the time they cook it, here are some ways food can be contaminated:

-They can have a food borne illness
-show symptoms of gastrointestinal illness
-have infected wounds
-are exposed to people who are ill
-touch anything that may contaminate food (Phone)

Personal Behavior That Can Contaminate Foods
-scratching scalp
-whipping or touching nose
-touching pimple or open sore
-wearing a dirty uniform
-rubbing or scratching ears
-running fingers threw hair
-sneezing into hand

4 Principals of Hand Washing
1. warm water(Above 100°F)
2. Soap
3. 20 Sec. Wash and Rinse
4. Drying hands (Single Use Towels)

When To Wash Your Hands
-after touching your hair
-using restrooms
-handling raw food
-sneezing, coughing
-touching soil clothes
-cleaning tables
-smoking, eating, drinking
-handling garbage
-handling chemicals

Food Borne Illnesses

Food Borne Infection
-A disease resulting from
Eating food containing
Live microorganisms
(salmonellas, shigellosis,
Listerioss)

Food Borne Intoxication
-A disease resulting from
eating food containing
toxins or poisons from
live/dead microorganisms
(staphylococcus, Boutolism)

There are four types of microorganisms that can be contracted threw food and cause food borne illnesses, they are:
-Bacteria
-Viruses
-Parasites
-Fungi

Basic Characteristics of Bacteria
-living, single-celled
-can be carried by food, humans, insects, etc.
-can reproduce rapidly
-certain types of bacteria can survive freezing

-bacteria can form spores which allow them to survive rough temperatures
-some can spoil food, others can cause illnesses
-most produce toxins that cause illnesses
-bacteria doubles every 20min.

Bacteria is a <u>pathogen</u>: A disease causing microorganisms

Growth Conditions of Bacteria

F	**A**	**T**
Food	Acidity	Time
T	**O**	**M**
Temperature	Oxygen	Moister

Controlling Growth

-make food more acidic
-raise or lower temperature
-lower foods water activity
-minimize time food spends in danger zone

Basic Characteristics of Viruses
-unlike bacteria, viruses rely on living cells
-unlike bacteria, they do not reproduce in food
-some types of viruses survive freezing or cooking
-can be transmitted person to person
-can contaminate food and/or water

Basic Characteristics of Parasites
-living organisms that need a host to survive
-small, often microscoptic
-grow naturally in animals, can be transmitted to humans

-can be killed by cooking or freezing
-pose hazards to food and water

Characteristics of Molds and Yeast
-spoil food and cause illness
-grow well in sweet acidic foods
-freezing can prevent or reduce growth
-most produce toxins called allatoxins
-many produce a nauseating aroma

Food Borne Contaminations

Biological:
-seafood toxins
-plant toxins
-mushroom toxins
-bacteria, viruses

Physical:
-hair in salad
-fingernail
-cold sore

Chemical:
-metals
-cleaners
-detergents

Most Common Causes of Food Borne Illnesses (FBI)
- Undercooked Food
- Unsanitary Foods
- Left in Danger Zone For To Long
- Failing To Cook Food Properly
- Failure To Heat Food Properly
- Adding Raw Products To Cooked Food
- Preparing Food A Day In Advance

Identifying Food and Waterborne Illnesses
Viruses
Disease: Hepatitis A-Infection
Organism: Hepatitis A Virus
Symptoms: Minor Flu-Like to Liver Failure
Source: Fecal-Oral Contamination

Disease: Vital Gastroenteritis (Intestinal Flu)
Organism: Various Viruses (Norwalk Virus, Rotavirus, Etc)
Symptoms: Flue-Like
Source: Fecal-Oral Contamination

Disease: Creutzfeldt-Jakob Disease, Kuru (Mad-Cow Disease)
Organism: Prion
Symptoms: Dementia, Seizures, Inevitably Fatal
Source: Transplant, Cannibalism

Bacteria
Disease: Staphylococcal Food Poisoning
Organism: Staphylococcus spp-Bacteria
Symptoms: Vomiting, Diarrhea
Source: Contaminated Food Left At Room Temperature

Disease: Botulism
Organism: Clostridium Botulism
Symptoms: Paralysis, Respiratory Failure
Source: Improperly Caned Foods

Disease: E. Coli Infection
Organism: Escherichia Coli
Symptoms: Bloody Diarrhea, Potentially Fetal Hemolytic-Uremic Syndrome
Source: Undercooked Beef, Unpasteurized Milk

Disease: Typhoid Fever
Organism: Salmonella Typhi
Symptoms: Fever
Source: Fecal-Oral Contamination

Disease: Shigellosis
Organism: Shigella
Symptoms: Vomiting, Diarrhea
Source: Fecal-Oral Infection

Parasites
Disease: Giardiasis
Organism: Giardia Duodenalis
Symptoms: Diarrhea
Source: Contaminated Water

Disease: Trichinosis
Organism: Trichinella Spiralis

Symptoms: Muscle Cysts
Source: Undercooked Carnivore Meat

Disease: Anisakiasis
Organism: Anisakis Simplex
Symptoms: Vomiting, Worms In Throat
Source: Seafood

<u>Fungi</u>
Disease: Muscarine Poisoning
Organism: Clitocybe
Symptoms: Vomiting, Diarrhea, Convulsions
Source: Toadstool

Disease: Phalloidine
Organism: Amanita Phalloides
Symptoms: Liver Damage, Death
Source: Toadstool

Disease: Ergotism
Organism: Claviceps Purpurea
Symptoms: Cramps, Spasms
Source: Grain

Handling and Storing Food

Know that you have some understanding of the factors that can affect food before it even get to the table. Here are some guidelines which will aid in the preparation and serving of food, as well as some great insights on how to run a cleaner and safer kitchen.

Receiving/Purchasing Proteins

- Beef that has a bright cherry color is a good sign of fresh meat, it should not be sticky or have an odor. It should be individually wrapped/portion (Vacuum Sealed) that is a good indicator that it has not been tampered with
- Lamb should be light red to opaque, should have a clean smell and should not have silver skin (elastic connective tissue) lamb should feel soft but not overly soft that is a sign of age lamb

- Seafood should not have any type of smell or odor, if buying shellfish such as oyster or clams make sure that they are closed. An open bivalve is a sign of a dead clam or oyster. If pertaining to fish look for smooth shiny skin, with no odor, bright pink or light red gills, bright shiny eyes and firm texture
- Poultry should be smooth with no bruises and be slightly sticky not overly, should have a clean smell as well as have bright off pink color that is a good indication that poultry is fresh

Receiving/Purchasing Dairy and Dry Goods

- Eggs should not have any kind of odor, shells should be clean and unbroken. Conditions should be firm, stiff yolks and should not have any kind of sulfur smell or have cracked shells
- Cheese should be individually wrapped and package if soft cheese look for no signs of visible molds or spots that seem to soft, if hard cheese avoid cheeses that have dark edges that's an indicator of freezer burn. Cheese should have smooth texture regardless if it's a soft cheese or hard cheese
- Milk products such as cream or half and half should be cold to the touch and have no signs of tampering, and should not be lumpy. Generally milk products have a 3 to 5 day buffer zone from their expiration date
- Dry goods such as pastas should be sealed and not be damage or broken, should have a soft feel and shinny texture with no mold present

The Flow Of Food
Always remember FIFO (First in First Out)

FIFO is an important tool that any culinarian should know, FIFO is a simple acronym meaning First in First out, this refers to the position of food as it is rotated in any kitchen. The best way to keep up with food rotation is to label all foods, once you open it you should label it and in some cases once you open a product you should refrigerate to keep it from spoiling.

Whether its cold food, hot food or dry storage food, it is important to follow proper protocol and procedures, the most important is time and temperature management, if food is cooked and is going to be held it should be held at 135°F. and if food is going to be stored cool it should be stored at or below 41°F. food that is going to left out should also be in a cool place at a temperature of 50°F to 75°F. Food can be left out in what is called the danger zone (41°F-135°F) for a maximum of 4hrs. Any more and the food will spoil, as the average bacteria doubles every 20 min. food that is kept at 135°F or higher can only be reheated once after it has been cooked because even do cooking kills the bacteria it does not kill the toxins that bacteria produce.

Cooling food can have the same effect once you freeze a product you cannot refreeze it because bacteria is still present, and they form spores which allow them to survive even the coldest temperatures. Food that is placed in a dry storage area can also be affected that's why the preferable temperature is below 75°F to prevent moister which is one key ingredient that bacteria thrive on. One of the effective measures that you can take when preparing food is a standard thermometer, a thermometer comes in handy when determining whether the product being used is safe and out of the danger zone, a typical thermometer is accurate up to 2°F of the projected temperature. The best way to make sure your thermometer is accurate is to calibrate it, there are two ways to do this the first is the boiling method which requires you to heat water to 212°F the boiling point of water and place your thermometer in and check the reading. The second and most commonly used is the ice method because it is faster and you don't run the risk of burning yourself, fill a cup with ice and water then place in thermometer it should read 32°F the temperature at which ice is formed. Most thermometers come with a built in wrench that are used to move the dial and calibrate the thermometer.

After understanding the precautions that need to be taken before you even start to prepare food, you will gain more insight on how taking the right measures can make your dining experience more pleasurable.

Conversion Specks

These are standards on which measurements are based on, how to convert ounces to grams, pounds to kilos. What you need to successfully convert any type of recipe specs are found below along with some conversion exercise.

1 Lb. = 0.45 Kg	32 F. = 0 C.
1 Kg = 2.205 Lb	39 F. = 3.89 C.
750 Ml = 25.5 Oz.	100 F. = 37.78 C.
1 Oz. = 28.35 g.	140 F. = 60 C.
1 g. = 0.035 Oz.	180 F. = 82.2 C.

1 Fl Oz. = 29.57 Ml	220 F. = 104 C.
1 Ml = 0.034 Fl Oz.	280 F. = 138 C.
3 Tsp. = 1 Tbsp.	300 F. = 148 C.
4 Tbsp. = 2 oz.	350 F. = 176 C
8 Tbsp. = ½ C.	0 F. =-18 C.
16 Tbsp. = 1 C. = 8 Oz.	128 oz = 1 G
2 C. = 1 Pint. = 16 Oz.	256 Tbsp = 1 G
4 C. = 2 Pint. = 1 Qrt. = 32 Oz.	768 Tsp = 1 G
8 C. = 4 Pint. = ½ G. = 64 Oz.	
16 C. = 8 Pint. = 4 Qrt. = 1 G. = 128 Oz.	
16 Oz. = 1 Lb.	

Conversion Exercise

1.) 2 gal. _____pts. 2.) 96 tsp._____ cups 3.) 80 oz._____ lbs.

4.) 9 qts. _____oz. 5.) 46 pts. _____qts. 6.) 96 oz._____ cups

7.) 5 gal. _____oz. 8.) 8 Tblsp._____ tsp. 9.) 4 gal. _____cups

10.) 3 pts. _____oz. 11.) 16 qts. _____gal. 12.) 48 qts._____ gal.

13.) 15 tsp._____ oz. 14.) 37 Tblsp._____ oz. 15.) 4 pts. _____Tblsp

16.) 48 tsp. _____pts. 17.) 3 gal. _____cups 18.) 1 gal. _____tsp.

Types Of Kitchen Cutlery

In the fast paste world of culinary arts there is a need to have the best of the best when it comes to purchasing cutlery. Some key notes to take into consideration are maintenance (how often you need to sharpen or hone your knife) cost (is it worth buying a knife that cost $150 appose to one that cost $20 and if so what the difference?). Knifes are molded by pressing steel into molds to shape the knife and sharpen with diamond blades, the difference between a $20 knife and a $150 knife can be a number of things weather you like the name brands or not, if you like a heavy knife appose a lighter one. The differences are simple but that is what makes a knife unique some can be forged from single steel plates and others can be layered from different types of material according to the consumers request. The best way to find the right knife for you and your needs is threw feeling how does the knife make you feel when you hold it, does it make you feel confident does it move the way you would like it to, and finally do you see yourself using it everyday. Over the years I have found that price doest not matter I personally own many knives that are between the ranges $20 and $150 and I have found that they all work best for me because of the feeling I have when I hold them, here are a some typical knives and their descriptions that can be found in any basic kitchen.

Note: not all kitchen cutlery is described below, these are a few of many knives that can be found

Chef Knife (French Knife)
This is the most important knife a cook can have. This all purpose knife is used for a variety of cutting and chopping work, as well as slicing and mincing. The blade is normally 8 to 12 inches long and a few inches wide.
A good Chef Knife in the hands of a skilled cook can be more accurate and faster than a machine.
Utility Knife
This smaller, lighter knife is used for light cutting and slicing jobs, often on fruits and vegetables.
The blade is usually 5 or 6 inches long.
Bread Knife
For slicing breads, cakes and pasteries, a bread knife is used most often in the bakeshop and to cut loaves of crusty bread.
The blade is usually 8 to 10 inches long.
Boning Knife

Used for separating raw meat from the bone. It has a thin short blade and is often stiff or flexible.

The blade is usually 5 or 6 inches long.

Filleting Knife

Used for filleting fish. It has a thin flexible blade.

The blade is usually 6 or 10 inches long.

Carving Knife (slicer)

Used for carving large roasts, turkey and also filleting very large fish. It has a long slightly flexible blade.

The blade is usually 10 to 14 inches long.

Cleaver

Used for chopping meats and cutting through bones. It has a heavy rectangular blade.

Not to be confused with the Chinese Cleaver (a Chinese Chef Knife) used for most cutting and chopping.

The blade is usually 10 to 14 inches long.

Paring Knife

Used for For peeling, slicing, trimming and dicing small fruits, vegetables and cheese.

The blade is usually 3 to 4 inches long.

Tourne Knife (peeling)

Used for peeling, slicing, trimming and dicing small fruits, vegetables and cheese.

The blade is usually 2 to 3 inches long.

Steak Knife

Used for cutting steak, chicken and other main courses.

The blade is 4 to 5 inches long and can be wide or thin, serrated or smooth.

Clam Knife

Used for opening clams.

The blade is 3 to 4 inches long and slightly sharp, it should be used with a butchers glove.

Oyster Knife

Used for opening oysters.

The blade is 3 to 4 inches long and blunt, it should be used with a butchers glove.

Sharpening Steel

Used for retruing or re aligning the knife edge. It should be used after each cutting task, several strokes on both sides of the blade holiding the knife at a 20 degree angle.

Sharpening Steels are 10 to 14 inches long.

Diamond Sharpening steels are faster and save time compared to a traditional butchers steel.

Preliminary Knife Cuts

understanding what types of knife cuts to use is only the beginning, most are just common sense but for those that are not here are some common knife cuts and their descriptions.

Chiffonade: Finely sliced or shredded leafy vegetables or herbs such as basil, mainly used in cold preparations

Chop: Cut of an irregular shaped pieces which can include: Rough Chop like in a Miropoix, Fine Chop or minced like in herbs, shallots, parsley, etc.

Mince: Fine chop of herbs or other type of flavoring ingredient such as garlic or shallots

Concassé: Generally used to described a diced, peeled and seeded tomato, can be any type of produced that has been seeded and peeled

Oblique: (Roll Cut) this is a two angle sided cut they vary in angles, lengths and diameters, usually used for cylinder vegetables such as celery, carrot and rapine

Rondelle: A round or bias round cut, varied in thickness and diameter

Julienne: The most commonly known cut is 2 inches long X1/8 X 1/8 in

Slice: These are cuts of uniform and relatively broad thin slices, usually used as garnishes or in soups

Flute: A unique decorative cut usually reserved for mushroom caps through making a series of shallow and curved grooves on the cap

Gaufrette: A waffle cut decorative slice made by using a mandolin

Parisienne: Uniform balls of fruit or vegetables that are created by using a parisienne scoop (Melon Baller)

Zest: The outer portion of the skin that is grated and used as a garnish or key ingredient

Tourné: A 2 inch long, ¾ inch in diameter, with seven equal sides and flat ends

Paysanne: ½ X ½ X 1/8 inch round, square or triangle

Large Dice: ¾ X ¾ X ¾ inch cube

Medium Dice: ½ X ½ X ½ inch cube

Small Dice: ¼ X ¼ X ¼ inch cube

Brunoise: 1/8 X 1/8 X 1/8 inch cube

Fine Bruinoise: 1/16 X 1/16 X 1/16 inch cube

Bâtonnet: 2 inch long X 1/8 X 1/8 inch

Gastronomy Terminology And Recipes

Gastronomy has been slowly making its way into the culinary industry, mixing chemicals into food seems to be the norm no a days probably because people have know just begun to understand its place in food. Gastronomy helps with the preparation and storing of food, now chefs have taken it one step further by introducing these chemicals into their daily routine and know you can to here are a couple of terms and definition along with some recipes to better help you understand the world of Gastronomy.

Acacia/Arabic Gum-Because Gum Arabic is such a versatile hydrocolloid, it has many applications. A superior emulsifier, our Gum Arabic Powder is widely used. Its low viscosity and adhesive properties make Gum Arabic an excellent ingredient for coating confections, and snack foods. For bakery products, the gum's binding and emulsification abilities aid in the formulation of icings and frostings as well as baked goods like cakes and pastries

Agar Agar-Agar is used at concentration of 1% or less. Sprinkle agar in hot solutions (175ºF) stirring well for several minutes. It is recommended to to premix agar with 1 to 3 times the weight of sugar or another powder. Gel will form on cooling

Calcium Chloride-For instant and irreversible gelling. Use in conjunction with Sodium Alginate to create "pearls" soft skin and other recipes for "Molecular Gastronomy".

Calcium Lactate-is a white crystalline salt used as a solidifier in molecular gastronomy. It is one of the most common forms in which calcium is found. It is made by the action of lactic acid on calcium carbonate; also used as a baking powder. Calcium lactate is also often found in aged cheeses. Small crystals of it precipitate out when lactic acid is converted into a less soluble form by the bacteria active during the ripening process

Carrageenan-Carrageenan is food approved in the US as an additive with gelling, stabilizing, and thickening properties. It is also use for freeze/thaw stability. Carrageenan is soluble in hot water (160ºF and should reach melting temperature of 175ºF for best results.

Onset temperature depends on salts and purity: typically between 100°F and 140°F

Dehydrated Apple Powder-These powders can used in combination with sugar to produce a perfectly colored coating for fruit jellies and in sauces were a boost of flavor without the addition of liquid is necessary. They are useful in candy fillings, desserts, breakfast cereals, yogurt flavoring and in any application where a fresh fruit flavor is desired. These fruits are processed to retain as much of their natural goodness as possible

Dehydrated Grapefruit Powder-processed using a refrigerated vacuum drier, which retains the natural color, flavor, nutritional value and particle size of the fresh fruit. Whole apples are then powdered retaining all the intense flavor of the fruit

Glycerol Monostearate-Widely used in food preparation, glycerol monostearate for emulsification, dispersion, foaming, and control of fat agglomeration Used in the preparation of ice-cream, sorbet, and confections where it allows aromas to develop. Recommended dosage for ice-cream preparations: .1% to .3% of final product weight. Caramels: .5% to 1% in weight. Lipophilic non-ionic surfactant with HLB of 3.6—4.2

Methylcellulose-thickener and emulsifier. Methylcellulose is a compound derived from cellulose. This white hydrophilic powder dissolves **ONLY** in cold liquid to form a clear viscous solution or gel. A solution of methylcellulose will turn solid when heated and since it is completely thermo-reversible will turn back to liquid when cooled. It is also used as a stabilizer in ice cream to help prevent the formation of ice crystals during freezing or re-freezing after a thaw. Like cellulose this component is non toxic, and not allergenic

Premium Macha Tea-One of the finest Green Tea imported directly from Japan, this macha green tea has a delicate flavor ideal for all your truffles, bonbons and/or ice cream preparation. Blend or mix into hot milk or cream to get it smooth and let infuse

Rennet-natural complex of enzymes produced in any mammalian stomach to digest the mother's milk. Rennet contains a proteolytic enzyme (protease) that coagulates the milk, causing it to separate into solids (curds) and liquid (whey).

Sodium Alginate-Alginates are used to prepare "fruit caviar" using fruit purees in an original solid yet soft "skin" also describe as "fruit pearls". Sodium alginate can be used below 1% as thickeners, binding and gelling agents. For instant and irreversible gelling, use 1% Calcium Chloride and above (up to 4% for "pearls", meat casings ...)

Sodium Citrate-Used in molecular gastronomy as a sequestering agent, sodium citrate attaches to calcium ions in water, keeping them from starting an early gelifying process

Sorbitol-compound naturally found in many fruits and berries and synthesized from glucose. It is widely used as a moisture-stabilizing agent in production of confectionery but also in baked goods and chocolate. Sorbitol prevents brittleness and excess of drying. It may also replace sugar when preparing reduced calorie recipes

Soy Lecithin-emulsifier added to chocolate bars to keep cocoa mass and cocoa butter from separating. It is used in numerous other applications requiring a natural emulsifier and/or lubricant. This Lecithin is extracted from soybean oil and comes in low viscosity liquid form, making it easier to add to an emulsion than granules.

Tapioca Maltodextrin-modified food starch that thickens and stabilizes fatty compounds. Used by pastry chef Alex Stupak of Alinea to turn peanut butter in granular powder form that reconstitutes instantly in your mouth.

Xanthan Gum-Xantham is used to stabilize suspensions, emulsions and foams. Excellent suspension for oil droplets in hollandaise, dressings and sauces

Lobster Gelee
200 g. Reduced Lobster Stock
.5 g. Agar Agar
TT Salt/White Pepper

Season the lobster stock and whisk in the
Agar Agar, Bring to a simmer and allow to
Cool for 2 hr. in refrigerator.

Strawberry Champagne Gelatin
500 ml. Strawberry Champagne
3 ea. Gelatin Sheets
1 g. Sugar

Bloom gelatin in ice water and add to sauce pot
With champagne and sugar, bring to a simmer
Stirring occasionally. Remove from heat and allow
To cool for 2 hr. in refrigerator.

Coco-Pineapple Foam
600 ml. Pineapple Juice
100 ml. Strawberry Juice
250 ml. Coconut Milk
50 ml. Pineapple Rum
10 g. Gelatin

Bloom the gelatin in ice water and add to sauce
Pot with the rest of the ingredients, bring to a
Simmer and remove from heat; add to 1L.
Whipper and charge with nitrous oxide. Let chill
For 2 hr. before dispensing.

White Grape Saffron Foam
70 ml. White Concord Grape Juice
430 ml. Manufacturing Cream
2 t. Saffron Threads

170 ml. Chablis
3.4 g. gelatin

Simmer Chablis and saffron threads over low heat
Add cream and grape juice and reduce by ¼. While
that's going bloom the gelatin and add to the
Mixture stir smooth and add mixture to 1L. Whipper
Loaded with nitrous oxide. Refrigerate for 3 hr.
Before use.

Tamarind Gummy's
200 ml. Tamarind Paste
2.5 Vanilla Beans
80 g. Caster Sugar
25 g. Glucose
10 g. Gelatin
100 ml. water
100 g. Isomalt

Bloom Gelatin and heat all ingredients to
Sauce pot and bring to a simmer, blend using
An emersion blender, let cool slightly and
Squeeze out excess liquid add to mold and let
Sit for 3 hr.

Strawberry Crème Anglace Ice Cream
400 ml. Crème Anglace
100 ml. Strawberry Sauce
100 ml. Nitrous Glycerin

Add Anglace to mixer and whip on lowest level,
Add the strawberry sauce and continue to whip
Until evenly incorporated; know slowly add the
Glycerin until Anglace Thicken, Serve Immediately.

Macaroni Consomme
230 g. Chicken Consomme
5.7 g. Gellan

Mix evenly and bring to a boil, transfer
To square container and allow to cool.
Slice thinly on mandolin and slowly roll
Close and from into macaroni.

Airy Key-Lime
200 g. Key Lime Juice
250 g. Water
1.2 g. Lecithin

Mix all ingredients together and let sit
For 1 min. and using an emersion blender
Whip the surface until aerated.

Raspberry Caviar
250 g. Raspberry Sauce
50 g. Raspberry Pucker
2.1 g. Sodium Alginate
500 g. water
2.5 g. Calcium Chloride

Mix the chloride with water and let stand, in a
Separate container mix all other ingredients
Until evenly incorporated. Add mixture to a
Dropper and drop on dot at a\time into the calcium
Mixture, strain and wash over running water.

Discovering Produce

Produce is the term given to farmed products that are sold for retail, generally limited to fruits and vegetables. The term "Produce" refers to foods that are fresh and generally grown in the same state or territory from which they are harvested. Produce is the main product sold by grocery stores, farmers and markets; many markets use codes to determine the quality and grade of produce one good example is the codes used by grocery store called Price Look-Up which are: 3 or 4 produce is conventionally grown with the use of pesticides and/or fertilizers. 9 produce is grown organically without pesticides. 8 GMO produce, contains genetically modified material. Although most produce can be available all year round it is always best to buy produce when its in season for that's when it is at its best and is often cheaper to buy. The seasons go as follows:

Spring: Typical fruits are mango, apricots, pineapple and strawberries. Spring vegetables are delicate cabbages, peas, baby lettuces, baby spinach, and watercress. Other types include rhubarb, potatoes, asparagus, artichokes and avocados.

Summer: These types include berries such as raspberries and blackberries as well as stone fruits like peaches, nectarines and summer vegetables include eggplant, beets, tomatoes and zucchini.

Fall: Produce include figs, pomegranate, apples and grapes. Vegetables include various types of cabbages like cauliflower, collards, broccoli and endive. Root vegetables include turnips, ginger, garlic, yams and parsnips. Winter Squash include butternut, pumpkin and acorns as well as corn and peas.

Winter: Fruits include oranges, lemons, grapefruit and clementines. Vegetables include harder cabbages like kale, raddicchio, leeks and Brussels sprouts. Also seasonal root vegetables include radishes, rutabaga and turnips and include some winter squash.

Fruits and Vegetables can be found in all shapes, sizes, colors and dimensions. there is hundreds of thousands of type of produce and millions of hybrids one great example of this is the Avocado although the Hass Avocado might be the most popular its only one choice that consumer have from about over 600 types and hybrids of Avocadoes. As technology grows so does the market for these unique types of produce. The best way to purchase the freshest produce is to be aware of the seasons and the small but noticeable signs, always check for bright shinny skin with no bruises, produce must be firm not hard or soft, if your buying melons or fruit look for the natural stem disconnection it should be smooth with no apparent tampering as to say no human interaction just a natural cut that is an indication that the product is just right. The smell should be light and fresh with no stench or hint of pesticides or vinegars. Weather it be fruit or vegetables produce has long been the stable for any household and that is not likely to change by any means regardless of science and biological interference. Here are a couple of my favorite types of produce including their variations and hybrids.

Tomatoes

BeefSteak-Bright Red and large tomatoes, usually used in foodservice for sandwiches or wedges for salads.

Cherry-The size of a small cherry, this tomato is bright red or yellow. Used mainly in salads for its sweetness.

Sweet 100's-A type of cherry tomato, this tomato is very sweet used in sauces and salads

Sungolds-These types of tomatoes are small, sweet and plump, they come in a variety of colors

Mini Charms-Small and tart these types of tomatoes are mainly used in cocktails

Grape-Petite in size these tomatoes are sweet and perfect for garnishing

On The Vine/Cluster-These are by far the smallest tomatoes you can buy, they are usually sold in clusters hence the name

Currant-The tinniest of the tomatoes these are very sweet and are usually bright red in flesh

Globe-Medium sized these tomatoes are good for slicing and eating raw

Heirloom-thin-skinned, highly perishable, antique varieties, (some are hundreds of years old)

Pear-These tomatoes resemble a tear drop, smaller than cherry tomatoes they are usually found yellow in color

Roma-These tomatoes are perfect for sauces because of the lack of juice and great fleshy texture

Striped-Orange in color with light red lines going across its flesh

<u>Eggplant</u>
Beauty-Oval shaped, glossy black color and about 25"

Black Beauty-Bushy top, nearly fully black in color, about 24"

Black Bell-Oval Fruit, Deep purple to black color

Black Jack-Light black color, used mainly for stir-fry

Classic-large oval shaped, perfect for roasting or stewing

Dusky-Glossy purple to black color, best if roasted

Imperial-Age 70 days, light black color, perfect for grilling

Little Fingers-slim in size about 4", grown in clusters

Casper-white color with purple tip. Sweet and tender

Thai-Small and round, about the size of a standard golf ball, reddish orange color

Summer & Winter Squash

Acorn-small and blue in color this squash, sweet and fibrous good for baking

Ambercup-Light orange color that resembles a pumpkin this squash has a sweet dry taste

Autumn Cup-Dark green in color with a rich fruit flavor

Banana-Bright orange with a sweet flesh often comes cut into smaller pieces

Butternut-Beige in color, this squash has a similar taste and texture to sweet potatoes, creamy sweet nutty flavor

Carnival-Cream in color with orange and green spots, thick skin only meat is edible, butternut taste

Hubbard-Large in shape with a slight grey color, of en sold in pieces this squash has a bold flavor

Spaghetti-Long and golden in color with a mild nutty flavor, when cooked flesh become strands that resemble spaghetti

Apples

Red Delicious-Bright red in color, mild flavor with a classic heart shape

Golden Delicious-Firm white flesh, mild flavored considered an all purpose apple, great for baking

Granny Smith-Tart in flavor whit bright green flesh, good for baking

Fuji-Sweet and tangy with a yellow-green flesh color best for pie's

Braeburn-Greenish-gold in color with a sweet taste perfect for salads

Pippin-Bright green very aromatic great for applesauce

Cameo-Sweet flavor with a firm with a cream-red tint, perfect for desserts

Understanding Beef

What is Beef?
The domestication of cattle for food dates to about 6500 B.C. in the Middle East. Cattle were not native to America, but brought to the New World on ships by European colonists. Americans weren't big eaters of fresh beef until about 1870, due to the enormous growth of the cattle industry in the West. The introduction of cattle cars and refrigerated cars on the railroad facilitated distribution of the beef.

"Beef" is meat from full-grown cattle about 2 years old. A live steer weighs about 1,000 pounds and yields about 450 pounds of edible meat. There are at least 50 breeds of beef cattle, but fewer than 10 make up most cattle produced. Some major breeds are Angus, Hereford, Charolais, and Brahman.

"Baby beef" and "calf" are 2 interchangeable terms used to describe young cattle weighing about 700 pounds that have been raised mainly on milk and grass. The meat cuts from baby beef are smaller; the meat is light red and contains less fat than beef. The fat may have a yellow tint due to the vitamin A in grass.

"Veal" is meat from a calf which weighs about 150 pounds. Those that are mainly milk-fed usually are less than 3 months old. The difference between "veal" and "calf" is based on the color of their meat, which is determined almost entirely by diet. Veal is pale pink and contains more cholesterol than beef.

NOTE: This information is about whole muscle beef and variety beef. See "Focus on Ground Beef" for information about hamburger and ground beef.

How are Cattle Raised?

All cattle start out eating grass; three-fourths of them are "finished" (grown to maturity) in feedlots where they are fed specially formulated feed based on corn or other grains.

Can Hormones & Antibiotics Be Used in Cattle Raising?

Antibiotics may be given to prevent or treat disease in cattle. A "withdrawal" period is required from the time antibiotics are administered until it is legal to slaughter the animal. This is so residues can exit the animal's system. FSIS randomly samples cattle at slaughter and tests for residues. Data from this Monitoring Plan have shown a very low percentage of residue violations. Not all antibiotics are approved for use in all classes of cattle. However, if there is a demonstrated therapeutic need, a veterinarian may prescribe an antibiotic that is approved in other classes for an animal in a non-approved class. In this case, no detectable residues of this drug may be present in the edible tissues of the animal at slaughter.

Hormones may be used to promote efficient growth. Estradiol, progesterone, and testosterone (three natural hormones), and zeranol and trenbolone acetate (two synthetic hormones) may be used as an implant on the animal's ear. The hormone is time released, and is effective for 90 to 120 days. In addition, melengesterol acetate, which can be used to suppress estrus, or improve weight gain and feed efficiency, is approved for use as a feed additive. Not all combinations of hormones are approved for use in all classes of cattle. Hormones are approved for specific classes of animals only, and cannot be used in non-approved classes.

How is Beef Inspected?

Inspection is mandatory; grading is voluntary, and a plant pays to have its meat graded. USDA-graded beef sold at the retail level is Prime, Choice, and Select. Lower grades (Standard, Commercial, Utility, Cutter, and Canner) are mainly ground or used in processed meat products. Retail stores may use other terms which must be different from USDA grades.

USDA Prime beef (about two percent of graded beef) has more fat marbling, so it is the most tender and flavorful. However, it is higher in fat content. Most of the graded beef sold in supermarkets is USDA Choice or USDA Select. The protein, vitamin, and mineral content of beef are similar regardless of the grade.

How Is Ungraded Beef Different?

All beef is inspected for wholesomeness. The overall quality of ungraded beef may be higher or lower than most government grades found in retail markets.

What is Marbling?

Marbling is white flecks of fat within the meat muscle. The greater amount of marbling in beef, the higher the grade because marbling makes beef more tender, flavorful, and juicy.

Retail Cuts of Fresh Beef

There are four basic major (primal) cuts into which beef is separated: chuck, loin, rib, and round. It is recommended that packages of fresh beef purchased in the supermarket be labeled with the primal cut as well as the product, such as "chuck roast" or "round steak." This helps consumers know what type of heat is best for cooking the product. Generally, chuck and round are less tender and require moist heat such as braising; loin and rib can be cooked by dry heat methods such as broiling or grilling.

Unfortunately, names for various cuts can vary regionally in stores, causing confusion over the choice of cooking method. For example, a boneless top loin steak is variously called: strip steak, Kansas City Steak, N.Y. strip steak, hotel cut strip steak, ambassador steak, or club sirloin steak.

How Much Beef Is Consumed?

Figures from the USDA's Economic Research Service show average annual per capita beef consumption for the following selected periods:

How Much Beef is Consumed?

Year	Weight	Year	Weight
1910-15	51 pounds	1960-65	69 pounds
1920-25	46 pounds	1970-75	85 pounds
1930-35	41 pounds	1980-85	78 pounds
1940-45	45 pounds	1990-95	67 pounds
1950-55	55 pounds	1995-97	64 pounds

Nutrition Labeling
Nutrition claims such as "lean" and "extra lean" are sometimes seen on beef products. Here are their definitions:

"Lean"—100 grams of beef with less than 10 grams of fat, 4.5 grams or less of saturated fat, and less than 95 milligrams of cholesterol.

"Extra Lean"—100 grams of beef with less than 5 grams of fat, less than 2 grams of saturated fat, and less than 95 milligrams of cholesterol.

What Does "Natural" Mean?
All fresh meat qualifies as "natural." Products labeled "natural" cannot contain any artificial flavor or flavoring, coloring ingredient, chemical preservative, or any other artificial or synthetic ingredient; and the product and its ingredients are not more than minimally processed (ground, for example). All products claiming to be natural should be accompanied by a brief statement which explains what is meant by the term "natural."

Some companies promote their beef as "natural" because they claim their cattle weren't exposed to antibiotics or hormones and were totally raised on a range instead of being "finished" in a feedlot.

How & Why is Some Beef Aged?
Beef is aged to develop additional tenderness and flavor. It is done commercially under controlled temperatures and humidity. Since aging can take from 10 days to 6 weeks, USDA does not recommend aging beef in a home refrigerator.

Why is Beef Called a "Red" Meat?
Oxygen is delivered to muscles by the red cells in the blood. One of the proteins in meat, myoglobin, holds the oxygen in the muscle. The amount of myoglobin

in animal muscles determines the color of meat. Beef is called a "red" meat because it contains more myoglobin than chicken or fish. Other "red" meats are veal, lamb, and pork.

Color of Beef
Beef muscle meat not exposed to oxygen (in vacuum packaging, for example) is a burgundy or purplish color. After exposure to the air for 15 minutes or so, the myoglobin receives oxygen and the meat turns bright, cherry red.

After beef has been refrigerated about 5 days, it may turn brown due to chemical changes in the myoglobin. Beef that has turned brown during extended storage may be spoiled, have an off-odor, and be tacky to the touch.

Iridescent Color of Roast Beef
Sliced cooked beef or lunch meat can have an iridescent color. Meat contains iron, fat, and many other compounds. When light hits a slice of meat, it splits into colors like a rainbow. There are also various pigments in meat compounds which can give it an iridescent or greenish cast when exposed to heat and processing. Iridescent beef isn't spoiled necessarily. Spoiled cooked beef would probably also be slimy or sticky and have an off-odor.

Additives
Additives are not allowed on fresh beef. If beef is processed, additives such as MSG, salt, or sodium erythorbate must be listed on the label.

Dating of Beef Products
Product dating is not required by Federal regulations. However, many stores and processors may voluntarily date packages of raw beef or processed beef products. If a calendar date is shown, there must be a phrase explaining the meaning of the date.

Use or freeze products with a "Sell-By" date within 3 to 5 days of purchase
If the manufacturer has determined a "Use-By" date, observe it. This is a quality assurance date after which peak quality begins to lessen but the product may still be used. It's always best to buy a product before its date expires. It's not important if a date expires after freezing beef because all foods stay safe while properly frozen.

What Foodborne Organisms are Associated with Beef?

Escherichia coli can colonize in the intestines of animals, which could contaminate muscle meat at slaughter. *E. coli* O157:H7 is a rare strain that produces large quantities of a potent toxin that forms in and causes severe damage to the lining of the intestine. The disease produced by it is called Hemorrhagic Colitis and is characterized by bloody diarrhea. *E. coli* O157:H7 is easily destroyed by thorough cooking.

Salmonella may be found in the intestinal tracts of livestock, poultry, dogs, cats, and other warm-blooded animals. There are about 2,000 *Salmonella* bacterial species. Freezing doesn't kill this microorganism, but it is destroyed by thorough cooking. *Salmonella* must be eaten to cause illness. They cannot enter the body through a skin cut. Cross-contamination can occur if raw meat or its juices contact cooked food or foods that will be eaten raw, such as salad.

Staphylococcus aureus can be carried on human hands, nasal passages, or throats. Most foodborne illness outbreaks are a result of contamination from food handlers and production of a heat-stable toxin in the food. Sanitary food handling and proper cooking and refrigerating should prevent staphylococcal foodborne illness.

Listeria monocytogenes is destroyed by cooking, but a cooked product can be recontaminated by poor handling practices and poor sanitation. FSIS has a zero tolerance for *Listeria monocytogenes* in cooked and ready-to-eat products such as beef franks or lunchmeat. Observe handling information such as "Keep Refrigerated" and "Use-By" dates on labels.

Rinsing Beef

It isn't necessary to wash raw beef before cooking it. Any bacteria which might be present on the surface would be destroyed by cooking.

How to Handle Beef Safely

- **Raw Beef:** Select beef just before checking out at the register. Put packages of raw beef in disposable plastic bags, if available, to contain any leakage which could cross-contaminate cooked foods or produce. Beef, a perishable product, is kept cold during store distribution to retard the growth of bacteria.

- Take beef home immediately and refrigerate it at 40 °F; use within 3 to 5 days (1 or 2 days for variety meats such as liver, kidneys, tripe, sweetbreads, or tongue) or freeze (0 °F). If kept frozen continuously, it will be safe indefinitely.

- It is safe to freeze beef in its original packaging or repackage it. However, for long-term freezing, overwrap the porous store plastic with aluminum foil, freezer paper, or freezer-weight plastic wrap or bags to prevent "freezer burn," which appears as grayish-brown leathery spots and is caused by air reaching the surface of food. Cut freezer-burned portions away either before or after cooking the beef. Heavily freezer-burned products may have to be discarded for quality reasons. For best quality, use steaks and roasts within 9 to 12 months.

- **Ready-Prepared Beef:** For fully-cooked, take-out beef dishes such as Chinese food, barbecued ribs, or fast food hamburgers, be sure they are hot at pickup. Use cooked beef within 2 hours (1 hour if the air temperature is above 90 °F) or refrigerate it at 40 °F in shallow, covered containers. Eat within 3 to 4 days, either cold or reheated to 165 °F (hot and steaming). It is safe to freeze ready-prepared beef dishes. For best quality, use within 4 months.

Safe Defrosting
There are three safe ways to defrost beef: in the refrigerator, in cold water, and in the microwave. Never defrost on the counter or in other locations.
- **Refrigerator:.** It's best to plan ahead for slow, safe thawing in the refrigerator. Ground beef, stew meat, and steaks may defrost within a day. Bone-in parts and whole roasts may take 2 days or longer. Once the raw beef defrosts, it will be safe in the refrigerator for 3 to 5 days before cooking. During this time, if you decide not to use the beef, you can safely refreeze it without cooking it first.
- **Cold Water:.** To defrost beef in cold water, do not remove packaging. Be sure the package is airtight or put it into a leakproof bag. Submerge the beef in cold water, changing the water every 30 minutes so that it continues to thaw. Small packages of beef may defrost in an hour or less; a 3-to 4-pound roast may take 2 to 3 hours.
- **Microwave:.** When microwave defrosting beef, plan to cook it immediately after thawing because some areas of the food may become warm and begin to cook during microwaving. Holding partially-cooked food

is not recommended because any bacteria present wouldn't have been destroyed.

Foods defrosted in the microwave or by the cold water method should be cooked before refreezing because they may have been held at temperatures above 40 °F.

It is safe to cook frozen beef in the oven, on the stove, or grill without defrosting it first; the cooking time may be about 50% longer. Do not cook frozen beef in a slow cooker.

Marinating
Marinate beef in the refrigerator up to 5 days. Boil used marinade before brushing on cooked beef. Discard any uncooked leftover marinade.

Partial Cooking
Never brown or partially cook beef to refrigerate and finish cooking later because any bacteria present wouldn't have been destroyed. It is safe to partially pre-cook or microwave beef immediately before transferring it to the hot grill to finish cooking.

Liquid in Package
Many people think the red liquid in packaged fresh beef is blood. However, blood is removed from beef during slaughter and only a small amount remains within the muscle tissue. Since beef is about 3/4 water, this natural moisture combined with protein is the source of the liquid in the package.

Safe Cooking
For safety, the USDA recommends cooking hamburgers and ground beef mixtures such as meat loaf to 160 °F on a meat thermometer. However, whole muscle meats such as steaks and roasts may be cooked to 145 °F (medium rare), 160 °F (medium), 170 °F (well done). For approximate cooking times for use in meal planning, see the following chart compiled from various resources.

Times are based on beef at refrigerator temperature (40 °F). Remember that appliances and outdoor grills can vary in heat. Use a meat thermometer to check for safe cooking and doneness of beef.

Approximate
Beef Cooking
Times °F

Type of Beef	Size	Cooking Method	Cooking Time	Internal Temperature
Rib Roast, bone in	4 to 6 lbs.	Roast 325°	23-25 min./lb.	Medium rare 145°
Rib Roast, boneless rolled	4 to 6 lbs.	Roast 325°	Add 5-8 min./lb. to times above	Same as above
Chuck Roast, Brisket	3 to 4 lbs.	*Braise 325°	*Braise 325°	Medium 160°
Round or Rump Roast	2 1/2 to 4 lbs.	Roast 325°	30-35 min./lb.	Medium rare 145°
Tenderloin, whole	4 to 6 lbs.	Roast 425°	45-60 min. total	Medium rare 145°
Steaks	3/4" thick	Broil/ Grill	4-5 min. per side	Medium rare 145°
Stew or Shank Cross Cuts	1 to 1 1/2" thick	Cover with liquid; simmer	2 to 3 hours	Medium 160°
Short Ribs	4" long and 2" thick	*Braise 325°	1 1/2 to 2 1/2 hours	Medium 160°

**Storage Times
for Beef
Products**

Product	Refrigerator 40 °F	Freezer 0 °F
Fresh beef roast, steaks, chops, or ribs	3 to 5 days	6 to 12 months
Fresh beef liver or variety meats	1 or 2 days	3 to 4 months
Home cooked beef, soups, stews or casseroles	3 to 4 days	2 to 3 months
Store-cooked convenience meals	1 to 2 days	2 to 3 months
Cooked beef gravy or beef broth	1 or 2 days	2 to 3 months
Beef hot dogs or lunch meats, sealed in package	2 weeks (or 1 week after a "Use-By" date)	1 to 2 months
Beef hot dogs, opened package	7 days	1 to 2 months
Lunch meats, opened package	3 to 5 days	1 to 2 months
TV dinners, frozen casseroles	Keep Frozen	3 to 4 months

Canned beef products in pantry	2 to 5 years in pantry; 3 to 4 days after opening	After opening, 2 to 3 months
Jerky, commercially vacuum packaged	1 year in pantry Refrigerate 2 to 3 months	Do not freeze

Understanding Veal

Veal is often associated with international cuisines such as Italian, French, German, Swiss, Hungarian, and Czech. Home cooks enjoy preparing veal for special occasions or for casual dinners such as barbecues. Veal is either USDA or state inspected. Here are some facts about veal

What is Veal?
Veal is the meat from a calf or young beef animal. A veal calf is raised until about 16 to 18 weeks of age, weighing up to 450 pounds. Male dairy calves are used in the veal industry. Dairy cows must give birth to continue producing milk, but male dairy calves are of little or no value to the dairy farmer. A small percentage are raised to maturity and used for breeding

Calf: A calf is a young bovine of either sex that has not reached puberty (up to about 9 months of age), and has a maximum live weight of 750 pounds

"Bob" Veal: About fifteen percent of veal calves are marketed up to 3 weeks of age or at a weight of 150 pounds. These are called Bob Calves.

"Special-Fed" Veal: Special, milk-fed and formula fed veal calves usually are fed nutritionally balanced milk or soy based diets. These specially controlled diets contain iron and 40 other essential nutrients, including amino acids, carbohydrates, fats, minerals and vitamins. The majority of veal calves are "special-fed."

How are Veal Calves Housed?
Today's modern, environmentally controlled veal barns provide for animal health and safety. The barns are lighted artificially and by natural light, and a constant source of fresh air is circulated.

Individual stalls are used for each calf. These stalls provide a safe environment where the calves can stand, stretch, groom themselves and lay down in a natural position. These pens are invaluable to the health of the animal. They allow the calves to be individually looked after. The stall's slotted floors allow for efficient removal of waste

How are Veal Calves Raised?

Veal calves are observed individually and are provided with specialized care. They also receive a milk replacer diet that provides all of the 40 vitamins and minerals they require.

Veal calves are usually separated from the cows within 3 days after birth, allowing for control of diseases and monitoring the dairy cow for udder problems.

Individual stalls allow veal farmers and veterinarians to closely monitor the health of each calf and properly treat a calf with a specific, government approved antibiotic. Veal farmers monitor each calf for health deficiencies such as anemia. The feed is controlled to meet the calves' iron needs. Health products for use with veal calves are approved by the Food and Drug Administration within the Department of Health and Human Services before being put on the market. The FDA also regulates information on the labeling of the product, the doses permitted, and withdrawal period

How is Veal Inspected?

All veal in retail stores is either USDA inspected for wholesomeness or inspected by State systems which have standards equal to the Federal government. Each calf and its internal organs are inspected for signs of disease. These inspections insure the veal is safe, wholesome, and correctly labeled and packaged.

Is Veal Graded?

Veal and calf carcasses are graded on a composite evaluation of two general grade factors: conformation (proportion of lean, fat, and bone in carcass); and quality of the lean. In addition, the color of the lean carcasses is key in differentiating between veal, calf and beef carcasses.

There are five grades for veal: prime, choice, good, standard, utility.

Grading is voluntary; a plant pays to have its meat graded.

When veal is graded, a shield-shaped purple mark is stamped on the carcass. With today's close trimming at the retail level, however, you may not see the USDA grade shield on the meat cuts at the store. Instead, retailers put stickers with the USDA grade shield on individual packages of meat. In addition, grade shields and inspection legends may appear on bags containing larger wholesale cuts

Are Hormones and Antibiotics Used in Veal Raising?

Antibiotics may be given to prevent or treat disease in the veal calf. Penicillin is not used in calf raising: tetracycline has been approved but is not widely used.

No hormones are used in veal raising. While growth-promoting hormones are approved for use in ruminating cattle, they have never been approved for use in non-ruminating veal calves.

Is Clenbuterol Used in the Raising of Veal Calves in the United States?

The use of Clenbuterol to raise veal calves is illegal in the United States. Clenbuterol is not a hormone, but a growth-promoting drug in the beta-agonist class of compounds.

Clenbuterol residues can affect lung and heart function in persons who have eaten liver or meat of animals given the drug. USDA considers any residue of Clenbuterol in meat unacceptable because of this. At the present time there have been no reported cases of illness related to Clenbuterol in the United States.

Retail Cuts of Fresh Veal

There are seven basic major cuts into which veal is separated: leg (round), sirloin, loin, rib, shoulder, foreshank and breast. When examining a package of veal, the label can help the purchaser identify the cut of meat in the package.

For example, a label stating "veal rib chop" identifies the packaged meat as "veal," the primal or large wholesale cut from the "rib," and the name of the retail cut, "chop." This information helps consumers know what type of preparation method to use. The most readily available cuts of veal today include rib chops, loin chops, cutlets, veal for stew, arm steak, blade steak, rib roast, breast, shanks, and round steak.

How Much Veal is Consumed?

In 2004, Americans consumed about .41 lbs. of veal per person yearly, according to USDA's Economic Research Service (ERS). Veal consumption reached an all-time high of 8.6 lbs. per person in 1944. The last year consumption topped one pound per person was in 1988.

What Does "Natural" Mean?
All fresh meat qualifies as "natural." Products labeled "natural" cannot contain any artificial flavor or flavoring, coloring ingredient, chemical preservative or any other artificial or synthetic ingredient; and the product and its ingredients are not more than minimally processed (ground, for example). All products claiming to be natural should be accompanied by a brief statement which explains what is meant by the term "natural".

Color of Veal
Veal is classified as a "red" meat, but typical lean meat on a veal carcass has a grayish pink color. Typical calf carcasses have a grayish red color of lean meat.

Dating of Veal Products
Dating of veal is **not required** by federal regulations. However, many stores and processors may *voluntarily* date packages of raw veal or processed veal products. If a date is shown, there must be a phrase explaining the meaning of the date.

If a manufacturer has determined a "use by" date, observe it. This is a quality assurance date after which peak quality begins to lessen but the product may still be used. It is always best to buy a product before its date expires.

What Foodborne Organisms are Associated with Veal?
Escherichia coli can colonize in the intestines of animals, which could contaminate muscle meat at slaughter. *E. coli* O157:H7 is a rare strain that produces large quantities of a potent toxin that forms in and causes severe damage to the lining of the intestine. The disease produced by it is called Hemorrhagic Colitis and is characterized by bloody diarrhea. *E. coli* O157:H7 is easily destroyed by thorough cooking.

Salmonella is a bacteria that can cause diarrheal illness in humans and may be found in the intestinal tracts of livestock, poultry, dogs, cats and other warm-blooded animals. There are about 2,000 *Salmonella* species. Freezing doesn't kill this microorganism but it is destroyed by thorough cooking. *Salmonella* must be eaten to cause illness. They cannot enter the body through a skin cut

How to Handle and Store Veal Safely
Fresh veal is kept cold during distribution to retail stores. When shopping, put packages of veal in disposable plastic bags, to contain leakage which could cross contaminate cooked foods or produce that will be eaten raw such as salad. Take veal home immediately and refrigerate at 40 °F or below.

Use veal chops and roasts within 3 to 5 days, and ground veal or stew meat within 1 to 2 days.

You may freeze veal at 0 °F or below. If kept frozen, veal will be safe indefinitely, although the quality can be affected with extended freezing. For best quality use frozen veal chops and frozen roasts within 4 to 6 months and ground veal or stew meat within 3 to 4 months.

It is not important if a date expires after freezing veal because all foods stay safe while properly frozen.

Rinsing Veal
There is no need to wash raw veal before cooking. Any bacteria that might be present on the surface would be destroyed by cooking. Wet meat won't brown well

Safe Thawing
There are three safe methods to thaw veal: in the refrigerator; in cold water; and in the microwave. When thawing in the refrigerator, estimate 4 to 7 hours per pound for a large roast, 3 to 5 hours per pound for a small roast, and about 12 hours for 1-inch thick rib or shoulder chops. Ground veal defrosting time depends on the thickness of the package.

To defrost veal in cold water, do not remove packaging. Be sure the package is airtight or put it into a leakproof bag. Submerge the veal in cold water, changing the water every 30 minutes so it continues to thaw. Small packages of veal may defrost in an hour or less: a 3 to 4 pound roast may take 2 to 3 hours. When thawing in cold water or in the microwave immediately cook the veal. Never thaw on the counter or any other locations at room temperature.

Raw ground veal and stew meat should be used in 1 or 2 days. Other cuts of veal should be safe in the refrigerator for 3 to 5 days before cooking.

Foods defrosted in the microwave or by the cold water method should be cooked before refreezing because they may have been held at temperatures above 40 °F, where bacteria multiply rapidly.

It is safe to cook frozen veal in the oven or on the stove or grill without defrosting. Estimate one-third to one-half more cooking time depending upon the size of the meat. Broil frozen veal farther away from the heat source; preheat the skillet when pan-frying or pan-broiling. Do not cook frozen veal in a slow cooker

Marinating

Marinate veal in the refrigerator up to 5 days for chops, roasts or steaks. Veal cubes or stew meat can be marinated up to 1 to 2 days. Boil used marinade before brushing on cooked veal. Discard any uncooked leftover marinade.

Irradiation

Irradiation has not been approved for use on veal products.

Partial Cooking

Never brown or partially cook veal to refrigerate and finish cooking later because bacteria may still be present and not have been destroyed. It is safe to partially cook or microwave veal immediately before transferring to the hot grill to finish cooking.

Safe Cooking

For safety, USDA recommends cooking ground veal to a safe minimum internal temperature of 160 °F. However, whole muscle meats such as veal steaks, roasts, and chops may be cooked to 145 °F (medium rare), 160 °F (medium), or 170 °F (well done).

There are two basic methods of veal cookery: dry or moist heat. Tender cuts including leg, cutlets, veal patties, and rib or loin chops can be prepared by dry heating methods such as roasting, broiling, pan broiling, grilling or stir frying. Moist heat methods such as braising or simmering in liquid can also be used with these cuts.

Less tender cuts, such as cross cut shanks, stew meat, round steak and breast of veal, generally require moist heat cooking methods. By marinating and pounding less tender cuts to break down connective tissue, dry heating methods can be used. Refer to the following chart for approximate cooking times

Approximate
Veal Cooking
Times

Type of Veal	Size	Cooking Method	Cooking Time	Internal Temperature
Rib Roast	4 to 5 lbs.	Roast 325°	25 to 27 min/lb	Medium 160 °F
			29 to 31 min/lb	Well done 170 °F
Loin	3 to 4 lbs.	Roast 325° F	34 to 36 min/lb	Medium 160 °F
			38 to 40 min/lb	Well done 170 °F
Loin/Rib Chops	1" thick or 8 oz.	Broil/ Grill	7 min per side	Medium 160 °F
			8 to 9 min per side	Well done 170 °F
Cutlets	1/8" thick	*Pan fry	3 to 4 min	Medium 160 °F
	1/4" thick		5 to 6 min	
Arm/Blade Steak	3/4" thick 16 oz.	Broil/ Grill	7 min per side	Medium 160 °F
			8 min per side	Well Done 170 °F
Round Steak	1/4" thick	**Braise	30 min	160 °F
	1/2" thick		45 min	
Boneless Breast, stuffed	2 to 2.5 lbs	**Braise	1 1/4 to 1 1/2 hrs	160 °F

	4 to 4.5 lbs		2 to 2 1/2 hrs	
Cross Cut Shanks	1 1/2" thick	Cover with liquid; simmer	1 to 1 1/4 hrs	160 °F
Stew Meat	1 to 1 1/2" cubes/ pieces	Cover with liquid: simmer	45 to 60 min	160 °F

<u>Understanding Poultry</u>

History & Definitions

The chicken is a descendant of the Southeast Asian red jungle fowl first domesticated in India around 2000 B.C. Most of the birds raised for meat in America today are from the Cornish (a British breed) and the White Rock (a breed developed in New England). Broiler-fryers, roasters, stewing/baking hens, capons and Rock Cornish hens are all chickens. The following are definitions for these:

- *Broiler-fryer* a young, tender chicken about 7 weeks old which weighs 2 1/2 to 4 1/2 pounds when eviscerated. Cook by any method.
- *Rock Cornish Game Hen*—a small broiler-fryer weighing between 1 and 2 pounds. Usually stuffed and roasted whole.
- *Roaster*—an older chicken about 3 to 5 months old which weighs 5 to 7 pounds. It yields more meat per pound than a broiler-fryer. Usually roasted whole.
- *Capon*—Male chickens about 16 weeks to 8 months old which are surgically unsexed. They weigh about 4 to 7 pounds and have generous quantities of tender, light meat. Usually roasted.
- *Stewing/Baking Hen*—a mature laying hen 10 months to 1 1/2 years old. Since the meat is less tender than young chickens, it's best used in moist cooking such as stewing.
- *Cock or rooster*—a mature male chicken with coarse skin and tough, dark meat. Requires long, moist cooking.

Chicken Inspection

All chickens found in retail stores are either inspected by USDA or by state systems which have standards equivalent to the Federal government. Each chicken and its internal organs are inspected for signs of disease. The "Inspected for wholesomeness by the U.S. Department of Agriculture" seal insures the chicken is free from visible signs of disease.

Chicken Grading

Inspection is mandatory but grading is voluntary. Chickens are graded according to USDA Agricultural Marketing Service regulations and standards for meatiness, appearance and freedom from defects. Grade A chickens have plump, meaty bodies and clean skin, free of bruises, broken bones, feathers, cuts and discoloration.

Fresh or Frozen

The term *fresh* on a poultry label refers to any raw poultry product that has never been below 26 °F. Raw poultry held at 0 °F or below must be labeled *frozen* or *previously frozen*. No specific labeling is required on raw poultry stored at temperatures between 0-25 °F.

Dating of Chicken Products

Product dating is not required by Federal regulations, but many stores and processors voluntarily date packages of chicken or chicken products. If a calendar date is shown, immediately adjacent to the date there must be a phrase explaining the meaning of that date such as *sell by* or *use before*.

The use-by date is for quality assurance; after the date, peak quality begins to lessen but the product may still be used. It's always best to buy a product before the date expires. If a use-by date expires while the chicken is frozen, the food can still be used.

Hormones & Antibiotics

No hormones are used in the raising of chickens.

Antibiotics may be given to prevent disease and increase feed efficiency. A "withdrawal" period is required from the time antibiotics are administered before the bird can be slaughtered. This ensures that no residues are present in the bird's system. FSIS randomly samples poultry at slaughter and tests for residues. Data from this monitoring program have shown a very low percentage of residue violations.

Additives
Additives are not allowed on fresh chicken. If chicken is processed, however, additives such as MSG, salt, or sodium erythorbate may be added but must be listed on the label.

Foodborne Organisms Associated with Chicken
As on any perishable meat, fish or poultry, bacteria can be found on raw or undercooked chicken. They multiply rapidly at temperatures between 40 °F and 140 °F (out of refrigeration and before thorough cooking occurs). Freezing doesn't kill bacteria but they are destroyed by thorough cooking.

USDA's Food Safety and Inspection Service has a zero tolerance for bacteria in cooked and ready-to-eat products such as chicken franks or lunch meat that can be eaten without further cooking.

Most foodborne illness outbreaks are a result of contamination from food handlers. Sanitary food handling and proper cooking and refrigeration should prevent foodborne illnesses.

Bacteria must be consumed on food to cause illness. They cannot enter the body through a skin cut. However, raw poultry must be handled carefully to prevent cross-contamination. This can occur if raw poultry or its juices contact cooked food or foods that will be eaten raw such as salad. An example of this is chopping tomatoes on an unwashed cutting board just after cutting raw chicken on it.

Following are some bacteria associated with chicken:
- *Salmonella* Enteritidis may be found in the intestinal tracts of livestock, poultry, dogs, cats and other warm-blooded animals. This strain is only one of about 2,000 kinds of *Salmonella* bacteria; it is often associated with poultry and shell eggs.
- *Staphylococcus aureus* can be carried on human hands, in nasal passages, or in throats. The bacteria are found in foods made by hand and improperly refrigerated, such as chicken salad.

- *Campylobacter jejuni* is one of the most common causes of diarrheal illness in humans. Preventing cross-contamination and using proper cooking methods reduces infection by this bacterium.
- *Listeria monocytogenes* was recognized as causing human foodborne illness in 1981. It is destroyed by cooking, but a cooked product can be contaminated by poor personal hygiene. Observe "keep refrigerated" and "use-by" dates on labels.

Rinsing or Soaking Chicken
It is not necessary to wash raw chicken. Any bacteria which might be present are destroyed by cooking.

Liquid in Package
Many people think the pink liquid in packaged fresh chicken is blood, but it is mostly water which was absorbed by the chicken during the chilling process. Blood is removed from poultry during slaughter and only a small amount remains in the muscle tissue. An improperly bled chicken would have cherry red skin and is condemned at the plant.

How to Handle Chicken Safely

- **Fresh Chicken:** Chicken is kept cold during distribution to retail stores to prevent the growth of bacteria and to increase its shelf life. Chicken should feel cold to the touch when purchased. Select fresh chicken just before checking out at the register. Put packages of chicken in disposable plastic bags (if available) to contain any leakage which could cross-contaminate cooked foods or produce. Make the grocery your last stop before going home.

- At home, immediately place chicken in a refrigerator that maintains 40 °F, and use within 1 or 2 days, or freeze at 0 °F. If kept frozen continuously, it will be safe indefinitely.

- Chicken may be frozen in its original packaging or repackaged. If freezing longer than two months, over wrap the porous store plastic packages with airtight heavy-duty foil, plastic wrap or freezer paper, or place the package inside a freezer bag. Use these materials or airtight freezer containers to repackage family packs into smaller amounts or freeze the chicken from opened packages.

- Proper wrapping prevents "freezer burn," which appears as grayish-brown leathery spots and is caused by air reaching the surface of food. Cut freezer-burned portions away either before or after cooking the chicken. Heavily freezer-burned products may have to be discarded because they might be too dry or tasteless.

- **Ready-Prepared Chicken:** When purchasing fully cooked rotisserie or fast food chicken, be sure it is hot at time of purchase. Use it within two hours or cut it into several pieces and refrigerate in shallow, covered containers. Eat within 3 to 4 days, either cold or reheated to 165 °F (hot and steaming). It is safe to freeze ready-prepared chicken. For best quality, flavor and texture, use within 4 months.

Safe Defrosting

FSIS recommends three ways to defrost chicken: in the refrigerator, in cold water and in the microwave. Never defrost chicken on the counter or in other locations. It's best to plan ahead for slow, safe thawing in the refrigerator. Boneless chicken breasts will usually defrost overnight. Bone-in parts and whole chickens may take 1 to 2 days or longer. Once the raw chicken defrosts, it can be kept in the refrigerator an additional day or two before cooking. During this time, if chicken defrosted in the refrigerator is not used, it can safely be refrozen without cooking first.

Chicken may be defrosted in cold water in its airtight packaging or in a leak proof bag. Submerge the bird or cut-up parts in cold water, changing the water every 30 minutes to be sure it stays cold. A whole (3 to 4-pound) broiler fryer or package of parts should defrost in 2 to 3 hours. A 1-pound package of boneless breasts will defrost in an hour or less.

Chicken defrosted in the microwave should be cooked immediately after thawing because some areas of the food may become warm and begin to cook during microwaving. Holding partially cooked food is not recommended because any bacteria present wouldn't have been destroyed. Foods defrosted in the microwave or by the cold water method should be cooked before refreezing.

Do not cook frozen chicken in the microwave or in a slow cooker. However, chicken can be cooked from the frozen state in the oven or on the stove. The cooking time may be about 50% longer.

Stuffed Chicken
The Hotline does not recommend buying retail-stuffed fresh whole chicken because of the highly perishable nature of a previously stuffed item. Consumers should not pre-stuff whole chicken to cook at a later time. Chicken can be stuffed immediately before cooking. Some USDA-inspected frozen stuffed whole poultry MUST be cooked from the frozen state to ensure a safely cooked product. Follow preparation directions on the label.

Marinating
Chicken may be marinated in the refrigerator up to 2 days. Boil used marinade before brushing on cooked chicken. Discard any uncooked leftover marinade.

Safe Cooking
FSIS recommends cooking whole chicken to a safe minimum internal temperature of 165 °F as measured using a food thermometer. Check the internal temperature in the innermost part of the thigh and wing and the thickest part of the breast. For reasons of personal preference, consumers may choose to cook poultry to higher temperatures.

For approximate cooking times to use in meal planning, see the following chart compiled from various resources.

Approximate
Chicken
Cooking
Times

Type of Chicken	Weight	Roasting 350 °F	Simmering	Grilling
Whole broiler fryer+	3 to 4 lbs.	1 1/4—1 1/2 hrs.	60 to 75 min.	60 to 75 min*
Whole roasting hen+	5 to 7 lbs.	2 to 2 1/4 hrs.	1 3/4 to 2 hrs.	18-25 min/lb*
Whole capon+	4 to 8 lbs.	2 to 3 hrs	Not suitable	15-20 min/lb*
Whole Cornish hens+	18-24 oz.	50 to 60 min.	35 to 40 min.	45 to 55 min*
Breast halves, bone-in	6 to 8 oz.	30 to 40 min.	35 to 45 min.	10—15 min/side
Breast half, boneless	4 ounces	20 to 30 min.	25 to 30 min.	6 to 8 min/side
Legs or thighs	8 or 4 oz.	40 to 50 min.	40 to 50 min.	10—15 min/side
Drumsticks	4 ounces	35 to 45 min.	40 to 50 min.	8 to 12 min/side
Wings or wingettes	2 to 3 oz.	30 to 40 min.	35 to 45 min.	8 to 12 min/side

<u>Understanding Pork</u>

What is Pork?

Pork is the meat from hogs, or domestic swine. The domestication of "pigs" (immature hogs) for food dates back to about 7000 B.C. in the Middle East. However, evidence shows that Stone Age man ate wild boar, the hog's ancestor, and the earliest surviving pork recipe is Chinese, at least 2000 years old.

Hogs were brought to Florida by Hernando de Soto in 1525, and soon was America's most popular meat. In the 19th century—as America urbanized and people began living away from the farm, "salt pork"—pork that is prepared with a high level of salt to preserve it—became the staple food. Pork has continued to be an important part of our diet since that time.

Pork is generally produced from young animals (6 to 7 months old) that weigh from 175 to 240 pounds. Much of a hog is cured and made into ham, bacon and sausage. Uncured meat is called "fresh pork."

Can Antibiotics and Hormones Be Used in Pork Raising?
Antibiotics may be given to prevent or treat disease in hogs. A "withdrawal" period is required from the time antibiotics are administered until it is legal to slaughter the animal. This is so residues can exit the animal's system and won't be in the meat.

FSIS randomly samples pork at slaughter and tests for residues. Data from this monitoring program have shown a very low percentage of residue violations.

No hormones are used in the raising of hogs.

How is Pork Inspected?
All pork found in retail stores is either USDA inspected for wholesomeness or inspected by state systems which have standards equal to the federal government. Each animal and its internal organs are inspected for signs of disease. The "Passed and Inspected by USDA" seal insures the pork is wholesome and free from disease.

Is Pork Graded?
Although inspection is mandatory, its grading for quality is voluntary, and a plant pays to have its pork graded. USDA grades for pork reflect only two levels: "Acceptable" grade and "Utility" grade. Pork sold as Acceptable quality pork is the only fresh pork sold in supermarkets. It should have a high proportion of lean meat to fat and bone. Pork graded as Utility is mainly used in processed products and is not available in supermarkets for consumers to purchase.

What to Look For When Buying Pork
When buying pork, look for cuts with a relatively small amount of fat over the outside and with meat that is firm and a grayish pink color. For best flavor and tenderness, meat should have a small amount of marbling.

Retail Cuts of Fresh Pork
There are four basic (primal) cuts into which pork is separated: shoulder, loin, side and leg.

Shoulder
- Shoulder Butt, Roast or Steak
- Blade Steak
- Boneless Blade Boston Roast
- Smoked Arm Picnic
- Smoked Hock
- Ground Pork for Sausage

Side
- Spare Ribs/Back Ribs
- Bacon

Loin
- Boneless Whole Loin (Butterfly Chop)
- Loin Roast
- Tenderloin
- Sirloin Roast
- Country Style Ribs
- Chops

Leg
- Ham/Fresh or Smoked and Cured

How Much Pork is Consumed in America?
Figures from the USDA's Economic Research Service show average annual per capita pork consumption for the following selected periods:
- 1970: 48 pounds
- 1975: 39 pounds
- 1980: 52 pounds
- 1985: 48 pounds
- 1990: 46 pounds
- 1994: 50 pounds

What Does "Natural" Mean?
All fresh meat qualifies as "natural." Products labeled "natural" cannot contain any artificial flavor or flavoring, coloring ingredient, chemical preservative or any other artificial or synthetic ingredient; and the product and its ingredients are not more than minimally processed (ground, for example). All prod-

ucts claiming to be natural should be accompanied by a brief statement which explains what is meant by the term "natural."

Why is Pork a "Red" Meat?

Oxygen is delivered to muscles by the red cells in the blood. One of the proteins in meat, myoglobin, holds the oxygen in the muscle. The amount of myoglobin in animal muscles determines the color of meat. Pork is classified a "red" meat because it contains more myoglobin than chicken or fish. When fresh pork is cooked, it becomes lighter in color, but it is still a red meat. Pork is classed as "livestock" along with veal, lamb and beef. All livestock are considered "red meat."

Dating of Pork

Product dating (i.e. applying "sell by" or "use by" dates) is not required by Federal regulations. However, many stores and processors may voluntarily choose to date packages of raw pork. Use or freeze products with a "sell-by" date within 3 to 5 days of *purchase*. If the manufacturer has determined a "use-by" date, observe it. It's always best to buy a product before its date expires. *It's not important if a date expires after freezing pork because all foods stay safe while properly frozen.*

What Foodborne Organisms Are Associated With Pork?

Pork must be adequately cooked to eliminate disease-causing parasites and bacteria that may be present. Humans may contract trichinosis (caused by the parasite, *Trichinella spiralis*) by eating undercooked pork. Much progress has been made in reducing trichinosis in grain-fed hogs and human cases have greatly declined since 1950. Today's pork can be enjoyed when cooked to a medium internal temperature of 160 °F or a well-done internal temperature of 170 °F.

Some other foodborne micro-organisms that can be found in pork, as well as other meats and poultry, are *Escherichia coli*, *Salmonella*, *Staphylococcus aureus* and *Listeria monocytogenes*. They are all destroyed by proper handling and thorough cooking to an internal temperature of 160 °F.

Rinsing Pork

It isn't necessary to wash raw pork before cooking it. Any bacteria which might be present on the surface would be destroyed by cooking.

How to Handle Pork Safely
Raw Pork. Select pork just before checking out at the supermarket register. Put packages of raw pork in disposable plastic bags (if available) to contain any leakage which could cross contaminate cooked foods or produce. Take pork home immediately and refrigerate it at 40 °F; use within 3 to 5 days or freeze (0 °F).

Ready-Prepared Pork. For fully cooked take-out pork dishes such as Chinese food or barbecued ribs, be sure they are hot at pick-up. Use cooked pork within two hours (one hour if air temperature is above 90 °F) or refrigerate it at 40 °F or less in shallow, covered containers. Eat within 3 to 4 days, either cold or reheated to 165 °F (hot and steaming). It is safe to freeze ready prepared pork dishes. For best quality, use within 3 months.

Safe Defrosting
There are three safe ways to defrost pork: in the refrigerator, in cold water (in an airtight or leak-proof bag) and in the microwave. Never defrost on the counter or in other locations.

It's best to plan ahead for slow, safe thawing in the refrigerator. After defrosting raw pork by this method, it will be safe in the refrigerator 3 to 5 days before cooking. During this time, if you decide not to use the pork, *you can safely refreeze it without cooking it first.*

When microwave-defrosting pork, plan to cook it immediately after thawing because some areas of the food may become warm and begin to cook during microwaving. Holding partially cooked food is not recommended because any bacteria present wouldn't have been destroyed. *Foods defrosted in the microwave or by the cold water method should be cooked before refreezing because they potentially may have been held at temperatures above 40 °F.*

It is safe to cook frozen pork in the oven, on the stove or grill without defrosting it first; the cooking time may be about 50% longer. Use a meat thermometer to check for doneness. Do not cook frozen pork in a slow cooker.

Marinating
Marinate pork in the refrigerator in a covered container up to 5 days. Boil used marinade before brushing on cooked pork. Discard any uncooked leftover marinade.

Irradiation

Irradiation has been approved for use on pork by FDA and USDA/FSIS in low-doses (to control trichina). Treated pork would not be sterile and would still need to be handled safely. *Trichinella* could be alive but would be unable to reproduce. Packages of irradiated pork must be labeled with the irradiation logo as well as the words "Treated with Irradiation" or "Treated by Irradiation" so they would be easily recognizable at the store.

Partial Cooking

Never brown or partially cook pork, then refrigerate and finish cooking later, because any bacteria present wouldn't have been destroyed. It is safe to partially pre-cook or microwave pork *immediately* before transferring it to the hot grill to finish cooking.

Safe Cooking

For safety, the USDA recommends cooking ground pork patties and ground pork mixtures such as meat loaf to 160 °F. Whole muscle meats such as chops and roasts should be cooked to 160 °F (medium), or 170 °F (well done).

For approximate cooking times for use in meal planning, see the attached chart compiled from various resources. Times are based on pork at refrigerator temperature (40 °F). Remember that appliances and outdoor grills can vary in heat. Use a meat thermometer to check for safe cooking and doneness of pork.

Can Safely Cooked Pork Be Pink?

Cooked muscle meats can be pink even when the meat has reached a safe internal temperature. If fresh pork has reached 160 °F throughout, even though it may still be pink in the center, it should be safe. The pink color can be due to the cooking method or added ingredients.

Microwave Directions

- When microwaving unequal size pieces of pork, arrange in dish or on rack so thick parts are toward the outside of dish and thin parts are in the center, and cook on medium-high or medium power.
- Place a roast in an oven cooking bag or in a covered pot.
- Refer to the manufacturer's directions that accompany the microwave oven for suggested cooking times.
- Use a meat thermometer to test for doneness in several places to be sure temperatures listed above have been reached.

Home Storage of Fresh Pork

Product	Refrigerator 40 °F	Freezer 0 °F
Fresh pork roast, steaks, chops or ribs	3—5 days	4—6 months
Fresh pork liver or variety meats	1—2 days	3—4 months
Home cooked pork; soups, stews or casseroles	3—4 days	2—3 months
Store-cooked convenience meals	1—2 days	2—3 months
TV dinners, frozen casseroles	Keep frozen before cooking	3—4 months

FRESH PORK: Safe Cooking Chart

Internal temperature of safely cooked pork should reach 160 °F when measured with a meat thermometer.

Fresh Pork: Safe Cooking Chart

Cut	Thickness or Weight	Cooking Time

ROASTING: Set oven at 350 °F. Roast in a shallow pan, uncovered. Internal temperature: 160°—medium; 170°—well done.

Loin Roast, Bone-in or Boneless	2 to 5 pounds	20-30 minutes per pound
Crown Roast	4 to 6 pounds	20-30 minutes per pound
Leg, (Fresh Ham) Whole, Bone-in	12 to 16 pounds	22-26 minutes per pound
Leg, (Fresh Ham) Half, Bone-in	5 to 8 pounds	35-40 minutes per pound
Boston Butt	3 to 6 pounds	45 minutes per pound
Tenderloin (Roast at 425-450 °F)	½ to 1½ pounds	20 to 30 minutes total
Ribs (Back, Country-style or Spareribs)	2 to 4 pounds	1½ to 2 hours (or until fork tender)

**BROILING 4 inches
from heat or GRILLING**

Loin Chops, Bone-in or Boneless	¾-inch or 1½ inches	6-8 minutes or 12-16 minutes
Tenderloin	½ to 1½ pounds	15 to 25 minutes
Ribs (indirect heat), all types	2 to 4 pounds	1½ to 2 hours
Ground Pork Patties (direct heat)	½ inch	8 to 10 minutes

IN SKILLET ON STOVE

Loin Chops or Cutlets	¼-inch or ¾-inch	3-4 minutes or 7-8 minutes
Tenderloin Medallions	¼ to ½-inch	4 to 8 minutes
Ground Pork Patties	½ inch	8 to 10 minutes

BRAISING: Cover and simmer with a liquid.

Chops, Cutlets, Cubes, Medallions	¼ to 1-inch	10 to 25 minutes
Boston Butt, Boneless	3 to 6 pounds	2 to 2½ hours
Ribs, all types	2 to 4 pounds	1½ to 2 hours

**STEWING: Cover pan;
simmer, covered with
liquid.**

Understanding Game

What is Game?
Game are wild animals and birds. Farm-raised game are originally wild species of animals and birds that have been raised for sale under existing State regulations. Large native game animals living in America include antelope, buffalo, bear, caribou, deer, elk, moose, reindeer, and wild boar. Elsewhere in the world, even rarer varieties eaten by humans are camel, elephant, kangaroo, wild goats, wild sheep, zebra, and other species.

Small game animals include alligator, rabbit, squirrel, beaver, muskrat, opossum, raccoon, armadillo, porcupine, and other species.

Game birds include grouse, guineafowl, partridge, squab (young pigeon), quail, pheasant, wild ducks, wild geese, wild turkey, and other species. Rock Cornish hens–thought by many consumers to be game birds–are actually young domesticated chickens.

NOTE: Game species raised on farms under appropriate regulations can be sold. Wild game species, that can be legally hunted under Federal or State regulatory authority, **cannot be sold,** but can be harvested for personal consumption. If you have questions about the harvest of wild game species, contact your State fish and wildlife agencies, or the U.S. Fish and Wildlife Service for Federal regulations on migratory species.

Background on "Venison" Game Animals
In culinary terms, "venison" can be meat from deer, elk, moose, caribou, antelope, and pronghorn. However, when this meat is offered for sale, the name of the specific animal must be specified on the package label.

Deer live in woodlands all over Europe, Asia, northern Africa and America. There are many deer species of various sizes but all the males grow antlers. The meat is lean and has a gamey flavor that can be made milder if soaked overnight.

Elk meat tastes like mild (almost sweet) beef, with only a very faint venison flavor. Elk can be substituted equally for venison in most standard venison recipes. Elk are from North America, Europe, and Asia.

Moose is the largest member of the venison family standing about 6½ feet at the shoulder. It's native from North America. The meat is similar to elk.

Caribou (reindeer) are slightly larger than white-tailed deer. Both males and females have antlers. The meat is somewhat sweeter than other venison. They live primarily in North America and Siberia.

Antelope are currently farmed in Texas, where black buck and nilgai antelope, native to Africa, are allowed to roam on huge preserves. Males are called bucks, bulls, or stags; females, does or cows; and unweaned young are fawns or calves. Antelope meat is leaner, but similar in taste, to that of deer.

Pronghorn (once classified as "antelope") is the last survivor of a species native to North America, with the largest herd in Wyoming. Pronghorn meat is leaner, but similar in taste, to that of deer.

Other Game Animals

Bison (buffalo) is native to North America. Once about 60 million in number, bison were hunted almost to extinction by the 1890's. Currently there are more than 150,000 animals being raised across North America today.

Musk-ox is a heavy-set, shaggy-coated wild ox that lives in northern North America, the Arctic islands, and Greenland. The meat tastes similar to buffalo.

Collared Peccary (javelina) is a hoofed animal native to parts of Mexico, South America, and the southwest U.S. A substitute is fresh pork.

Rabbits sold for consumption in the U.S. are not North American cottontails, but are usually either crosses between New Zealand and Belgian varieties, Chinese rabbits, or Scottish hares.

Wild boar, along with feral (wild) hogs, are found in 23 states in the U.S. and are estimated to number over 2 million. Like our domestic swine, these animals are not native to North America, but were originally brought over from other continents. Originally domesticated and then released into the wild, these animals are now hybrids.

While some states have limited hunting seasons, most states consider them a nuisance and encourage hunting them for personal consumption.

Game Birds

The game bird industry in the U.S. raises millions of birds for sale to restaurants and direct to consumers. These include up to 10 million pheasants, 37 million quail (including 12 million Bobwhite), 4 million Chukar partridges, 1 million Mallard ducks, 200,000 wild turkeys, and several other bird species.

Wild Ducks—The Chinese were the first to raise wild ducks domestically for food. Today's domestic wild ducks are descendants of either the Muscovy or Mallard species. America's Long Island ducks are offspring of Peking ducks (a variety of Mallard) brought from China in the late 1800's. A young duck or duckling (usually under 8 weeks of age) has dark, tender meat and weighs about 3 ½ to 5 pounds. A mature duck is usually over 6 months of age and has tougher meat.

Goose—Geese were farm-raised in ancient Egypt, China, and India. Today's goose weighs between 5 and 18 pounds. A young bird of either sex ("goose" is the female of the species; "gander," the male) has tender meat, while a mature goose of either sex has tougher meat.

Guineafowl—This relative of the chicken and partridge, sometimes called a guinea hen or African pheasant, was thought to originate in Guinea, West Africa. A young guineafowl, about 11 weeks old, has tender meat, while a mature bird has tougher meat. Female guinea fowl are more tender than males. The meat is light red and slightly dry with a mild gamey flavor. Due to their small size—about 2 to 3 pounds, including giblets–guinea fowl are usually sold whole.

Partridge–There are no native partridge species in the United States. Most partridge in the market are from European or African varieties. The Grey partridge, a European species, was imported from Hungary and raised in England. Found as far away as the Middle East, this variety is sometimes called Hungarian partridge. Chukar is a partridge species from India.

Pheasant—Originally from Asia, the female of this medium-size game bird (weighing about 3 pounds) has more tender, plump, and juicy meat than the male, which weighs about 5 pounds. Young birds can be roasted, but older birds need moist heat because their flesh is drier and leaner.

Quail—American quail are known regionally by various names: Bobwhite, partridge, and quail (blue, California, mountain and Montezuma). American quail nest on the ground and are not related to the European quail of the partridge family. A ready-to-cook quail weighs about 3 to 7 ounces, including the giblets. Due to their small size, they are usually roasted and served whole. The meat is dark, but mild flavored.

Squab or Pigeon—This species originated in the Middle East and Asia, and is one of the oldest birds known to man. A squab is a young, immature pigeon about 4 weeks old. Because it is too young to fly, the meat is very tender. Squab usually weigh about 12 to 16 ounces, including giblets, and have dark, delicately flavored meat. They are usually stuffed whole and roasted. A pigeon has been allowed to mature and has tougher meat than a squab.

Wild Turkeys—Turkey is one of North America's native birds. The name "turkey" was originally applied to an African bird, now known as the guineafowl, which was believed to have originated in Turkey. When the Europeans came upon the American turkey, they thought it was the same bird as the African guinea fowl, and so gave it the name turkey, although the two species are quite distinct. Compared to their domestic counterparts, wild turkeys are leaner, less meaty, not as tender, and have a stronger flavor.

Are Game Animals Inspected by USDA?
Some game animals are inspected by USDA and others by the U.S. Food and Drug Administration (FDA). USDA's Food Safety and Inspection Service (FSIS) has mandatory inspection authority over all food products from cattle, sheep, swine, goats, horses, mules, and other equines, chickens, turkeys, ducks, geese, guineas, ratites (emu, ostrich, and rhea), and squab. This includes processed products containing more than 3 percent raw meat or 2 percent or more cooked poultry meat.

Additionally, FSIS does voluntary inspection of reindeer, elk, antelope, water buffalo, bison, migratory water fowl (birds that swim such as ducks and geese), game birds, and
rabbits.

FDA has jurisdiction over *imported* fish, buffalo, rabbits, venison, wild game, and all other foods not covered by the Federal meat and poultry inspection laws. Meat and poultry exported from another country must meet all safety standards applied to foods produced in the United States, and this must be verified annually.

How Are Game Farm Raised?

Game animals are either raised on farms or ranches. If ranch raised, the animals are allowed to roam at will over hundreds of acres, foraging off foliage. Farm-raised game live in more confined outdoor areas and are fed grains such as wheat, alfalfa, or corn. What the animal eats can affect the taste of the meat.

Game bird species are raised separately from each other. Some birds consider birds from other species as intruders and will kill them.

The chicks need a clean, healthy environment, free of predators and parasites, with lots of clean, fresh water, fresh air, and feed. They are kept in warm buildings with floors covered with litter made of pine shavings, rice or peanut hulls, sugarcane fiber, and ground corncobs. Game birds are fed a diet similar to domestic poultry, typically a low-fat mix which is higher in protein than that fed to chickens. The feed may contain corn, alfalfa meal, wheat, soybean, meat bone scrap, whey, fish meal, and a vitamin-mineral mix. The FDA regulates animal feed.

When they are a few weeks old, game birds may be transferred to flight cages, typically 130 feet long, 12 feet wide, and 6½ feet high, with a floor cover of natural vegetation. There they must be protected from weather extremes, predators, people, and themselves. Access to a shed protects them from the elements.

Are Hormones and Antibiotics Used in Game Animal Production?

Hormones are not used in raising game birds or game animals; however, antibiotics may be used.

Wild birds and waterfowl are susceptible to many diseases and parasites, especially where large numbers are being raised in relatively small areas. The FDA approves medications that can be used to treat food animals. Very few drugs have been approved for game birds. Those approved are administered in their feed or water. The drugs are either antibiotics or anti-parasitics.

The FDA has strict guidelines for the use of drugs in animal production. If a drug is given, it must be used according to its labeling. Almost all these drugs require a "withdrawal" period—usually up to 5 days—from the time it is administered until it is legal to slaughter the animal or bird. This is so residues will not be in the meat. FSIS randomly samples the meat at slaughter and tests for any drug residues.

What Foodborne Bacteria Are Associated With Game?

As with any perishable meat, poultry, or fish, harmful bacteria, such as *Salmonella* and *Escherichia coli*, can be found on raw or undercooked game. They live in the intestinal tracts of game, livestock, poultry, dogs, cats, and other warm-blooded animals, and must be eaten to cause illness. Foodborne bacteria cannot enter the body through a skin cut.

There are about 2,000 species of *Salmonella* bacteria. *Escherichia coli* can colonize in the intestines of animals, which can contaminate muscle meat at slaughter. *E. coli* O157:H7 is a rare strain that produces large quantities of a potent toxin that forms in and causes severe damage to the lining of the intestine. One disease produced by it is called Hemorrhagic Colitis and is characterized by bloody diarrhea. Another disease, Hemolytic Uremic Syndrome (HUS), can cause kidney failure in the very young. A similar illness, thrombotic thrombocytopenic purpura (TTP), may occur in adults.

Bacteria multiply rapidly in the "Danger Zone"—temperatures between 40 and 140 °F. Cross-contamination can occur if raw meat or its juices come in contact with cooked foods or foods that will be eaten raw, such as salad. Freezing does not kill bacteria. Cooking to 160 °F kills bacteria.

How Does Game Meat Differ from Domestic Meat?

Because their diets and activity levels are not the same as that of domestic animals and poultry, the meat of farm-raised game animals has a different flavor—stronger than domesticated species and milder than wild game. The factors that determine the meat's quality include the age of the animal (younger animals are more tender), the animal's diet, and the time of year the animal was harvested. (The best is in the fall, after a plentiful spring and summer feeding.)

Equally important is how the animal was handled in the field. The animal should be eviscerated within an hour of harvest, and the meat refrigerated within a few hours. Meat is damaged (and sometimes ruined) if it is not dressed, transported, and chilled properly.

In general, wild game is less tender than meat from domestic animals because the wild animals get more exercise and have less fat. Any fat is generally bad tasting and should be removed. For maximum tenderness, most game meat should be cooked slowly and not overdone. It can be cooked with moist heat by braising or with dry heat by roasting. Ways to keep game moist include basting, larding, or barding (see "Cooking Methods").

Are Game "Red" or "White" Meat?
Game birds are poultry and considered "white" meat. Because they are birds of flight, however, the breast meat is darker than domestic chicken and turkey (which stand a lot, but do little, if any, flying). This is because more oxygen is needed by muscles doing work, and the oxygen is delivered to those muscles by the red cells in the blood.

All game animals are "red" meat. One of the proteins in meat, myoglobin, holds the oxygen in the muscle, and gives the meat a darker color.

What Does "Natural" Mean?
All fresh meat qualifies as "natural." Products labeled "natural" cannot contain any artificial flavor or flavoring, coloring ingredient, chemical preservative, or any other artificial or synthetic ingredient. The product and its ingredients cannot be more than minimally processed (ground, for example). All products claiming to be "natural" should be accompanied by a brief statement explaining what is meant by the term "natural."

Some companies promote their game as "natural" because they claim the animals weren't exposed to antibiotics or hormones and were totally raised on a range instead of being "finished" in a feedlot.

Food Product Dating
Product dating is not required by Federal regulations. However, many stores and processors may voluntarily date packages of raw game or processed game products. If a calendar date is shown, there must be a phrase explaining the meaning of the date. It's not important if a date expires after freezing game because all foods stay safe while properly frozen.

How is Game Handled Safely?
FRESH GAME. Because the demand is not as high as for domestic meats, game is usually sold frozen in supermarkets. However, fresh game is sometimes available. Always select the meat just before checking out at the register. Put fresh game in a disposable plastic bag (if available) to contain any leakage that could cross-contaminate cooked foods or produce. Make the grocery store your last stop before going home.

At home, refrigerate game immediately at 40 °F or below. Cook or freeze (0 °F) game birds and ground game within 1 or 2 days; game animals, within 3 to 5 days. If kept frozen continuously, it will be safe indefinitely.

READY-PREPARED GAME. If picking up cooked game or other fully-cooked product from a restaurant or other foodservice outlet, be sure it is either hot or cold when you pick it up. Use hot food within 2 hours or cut it into several pieces and refrigerate in shallow, covered containers. Eat either cold or reheated to 165 °F (hot and steaming). It is safe to freeze ready-prepared game. For recommended storage times, see the chart.

Quantity to Buy
When buying large whole game birds, allow about 1 to 1½ pounds of raw product per person. For small game birds, such as quail, two whole birds per serving may be necessary. Raw boneless meat yields about 3 servings per pound after cooking. Estimate 3 to 4 ounces per person for fully-cooked products.

How Do You Reduce the "Gamey" Flavor?
The distinct game flavor of either birds or animals will be milder after soaking the meat overnight in the refrigerator in either a salt or vinegar solution.
- Salt solution—one tablespoon per quart of cold water
- Vinegar solution—one cup per quart of cold water

Use enough solution to cover the game completely. Discard the solution after soaking.

You can also marinate game to give it a savory flavor or to tenderize it. Always marinate it in the refrigerator (1 to 2 days for birds; 3 to 5 days for game animals). Boil used marinade before basting meat as it cooks or using as a sauce on the cooked meat. Discard any uncooked leftover marinade.

Cooking Methods
The tenderness of a particular cut of game is similar to the corresponding cut of domestically-raised meat or poultry. All game tends to be leaner than that of domesticated animals, which have been bred for tenderness and fat marbling. Overcooking can toughen game. You can use moist heat, basting, and larding or barding (inserting slivers of fat or wrapping in bacon) to help keep the meat tender during cooking. Fast searing over high heat can also work for smaller cuts, such as tenderloin medallions or rib chops.

Safe Defrosting
There are three safe ways to defrost frozen game: in the refrigerator, in cold water, and in the microwave. Never defrost on the counter. Whole birds or ground meat may take 1 to 2 days or longer to defrost in the refrigerator; roasts, several days. Once the raw poultry defrosts, it will be safe in the refrigerator an additional day or two before cooking. Meat and poultry thawed in the refrigerator **may be safely refrozen without cooking it first.**

To defrost game in cold water, do not remove store packaging. Be sure the packaging is airtight or put it in a leak-proof bag. Submerge the product in cold water, changing the water every 30 minutes. A whole game bird (3 to 4 pounds) or package of parts should defrost in 2 to 3 hours; larger amounts of game may take 4 to 6 hours.

When microwave-defrosting game, plan to cook it immediately after thawing because some areas of the meat may become warm and begin to cook during microwaving. Holding partially-cooked food is not recommended because any bacteria present would not have been destroyed.

Foods defrosted in the microwave or by the cold water method should be cooked before refreezing.

Partial Cooking
Never brown or partially cook game to refrigerate and finish cooking later because any bacteria present would not have been destroyed. It is safe to partially pre-cook or microwave game **immediately** before transferring it to a hot grill or other cooking appliance to finish cooking

Can Safely-Cooked Game Be Pink?

Cooked muscle meats can be pink even when the meat has reached a safe internal temperature. If fresh game has reached 160 °F throughout, even though it may still be pink in the center, it should be safe. The pink color can be due to the cooking method, smoking, or added ingredients such as marinades. Cook ground meats and other cuts of game meat such as chops, steaks, and roasts to 160 °F to ensure destruction of foodborne bacteria and parasites.

Whole game birds are safe cooked to a minimum internal temperature of 165 °F as measured with a food thermometer. Check the internal temperature in the innermost part of the thigh and wing and the thickest part of the breast. For reasons of personal preference, consumers may choose to cook poultry to higher temperatures. Approximate cooking times for use in meal planning are given on the chart below.

Approximate
Game
Cooking
Times

TYPE OF GAME	ROAST	GRILL/ FRY Direct heat	SMOKE Indirect heat*	BRAISE/ STEW In liquid; covered

**GAME
BIRDS:**

Whole bird, 4 to 6 lbs. (Do not stuff.)	350 °F 30 to 35 min./lb.	Not preferred	2½ hours	Not preferred
Breast or parts	350 °F 1 to 1¼ hrs.	20 to 40 min.	2 hours	60 to 75 min.
Whole small birds	350 °F 45 min.	30 min.	1 to 1½ hrs.	45 to 60 min.

**GAME
ANIMALS:**

Rib Roast, bone in 4 to 6 lbs.	325 °F 27 to 30 min./lb.	Not recom- mended	Not recom- mended	Not recom- mended
Rib Roast, boneless rolled 4 to 6 lbs.	32 to 38 min./lb.	Not recom- mended	Not recom- mended	Not recom- mended
Chuck Roast, Brisket 3 to 4 lbs.	Not recom- mended	Not recom- mended	Several hours	325° 2 to 3 hours
Round or Rump Roast 2½ to 4 lbs.	325 °F 35 to 40 min./lb.	18 to 25 min./lb.	2½ to 3 hours	325° 2 to 3 hours
Whole leg (boar, deer) 6 to 8 lbs.	375 °F 2 hours	Not recom- mended	3 to 4 hours	Not recom- mended
Tenderloin whole, 4 to 6 lbs.	425 °F 45 to 60 min. total	12 to 15 min./side	Not recom- mended	Not recom- mended
Tenderloin half, 2 to 3 lbs.	425 °F 45 to 60 min. total	10 to 12 min./side	Not recom- mended	Not recom- mended
Steaks, ¾ inch thick	Not recom- mended	6 to 7 min./side	Not recom- mended	Not recom- mended
Ground meat patties	Not recom- mended	6 to 8 min./side	Not recom- mended	Not applicable
Meat loaf, 1 to 2 lbs.	350 °F 60 to 90 min.	Not recom- mended	Not recom- mended	Not applicable

Stew or Shank Cross Cuts 1 to 1½ inch thick	Not recom- mended.	Not recom- mended	Not recom- mended	Cover with liquid; sim- mer 2 to 3 hours
Ribs, 4 inches	375 °F 20 min.	8 to 10 min./side	Not recom- mended	Parboil 1 hour; then grill or roast

Home Storage of Game

Product	Refrigerator 40 °F	Freezer 0 °F
Fresh game birds	1 to 2 days	6 months
Fresh game animal meat	3 to 5 days	6 to 9 months
Fresh organ meat (liver, heart, kidney, or tongue)	1 to 2 days	6 months
Cooked game; soups, stews, or casseroles containing them	3 to 4 days	2 to 3 months
Leftover take-out or restaurant food	3 to 4 days	2 to 3 months
Smoked game, Vacuum-sealed	2 weeks (or 1 week after "Use-By" date)	1 to 2 months
After opening	7 days	1 to 2 months
Canned game products (paté, soup, stew, etc.)	3 to 4 days after opening	2 to 3 months after opening
Before opening, 2 to 5 years in pantry.		

Understanding Seafood

Fresh Seafood

Purchasing

When buying fresh seafood, use your eyes, hands, and nose. The word "fresh" refers to seafood that has not been frozen. However, that's not to imply that "frozen" is bad. As a matter of fact, frozen seafood can be superior in quality to fresh seafood products, so base your purchase on product quality.

How can you determine the quality of fresh seafood in the store? First, look at the display. All fresh seafood should be held at 32 F, which is maintained by refrigeration and/or ice. Fresh seafood should feel cold to the touch, not cool.

Whatever the variety, whole fish have certain characteristics that indicate freshness.

Bright, clear, full eyes that are often protruding. As the fish loses freshness, the eyes become cloudy, pink, and sunken.

Bright red or pink gills. Avoid fish with dull-colored gills that are gray, brown, or green. Fresh fish should be free from slime.

Firm and elastic flesh that springs back when pressed gently with the finger. With time, the flesh becomes soft and will slip away from the bone.

Shiny skin, with scales that adhere tightly. Characteristic colors and markings start to fade as soon as a fish leaves the water.

Fillets and steaks should have firm and elastic flesh and a fresh-cut, moist appearance, with no browning around the edges. Filleted flesh separates if it is left too long in the case. The flesh should be translucent, light will shine through it. There should be little evidence of bruising or reddening of the flesh from retention of blood. Prepackaged steaks and fillets should contain a minimum of liquid. Seafood stored in liquid deteriorates quickly. All fresh fish should have no fishy or ammonia smell.

Shellfish may be sold live, cooked, or fresh shucked. The form depends on availability and the shellfish itself. Each form and species will have different quality signs to examine. Odor is one quality indicator that should be sweet and mild, not overly fishy for all fresh shellfish. This odor has been likened to a fresh sea breeze or seaweed.

The shells of live clams, oysters, or mussels should be tightly closed. If the shells gape slightly, tap them. They should close; discard any that do not. The shells of live shellfish should not be cracked and should look moist. Oysters should have one shell that is well cupped. When selecting soft-shelled clams, the "neck" will show movement when touched. The meats of fresh shucked clams, oysters, or mussels should be plump and covered with their liquor. Their liquor should be clear or slightly opalescent (slightly milky or light gray) and free of shell or grit.

Scallops are not sold live because they are highly perishable. Scallops are shucked at sea shortly after capture. Fresh scallop meats have a firm texture and distinct sweet odor. A sour or iodine smell indicates spoilage. The smaller bay and calico scallops are usually creamy white, though there may be some normal light tan or pink coloration. The larger sea scallops are also generally creamy white, though they may show some normal light orange or pink color.

Live crabs and lobsters should show leg movement, and the tail of lobsters should curl tightly underneath the body and not hang down when the lobster is picked up. Lobsters and crabs will not be very active if they have been refrigerated, but they should move at least a little bit. The shell of a soft-shelled crab will be soft, while the shell of crabs and lobsters should be hard.

Cooked lobsters or crabs in the shell should be bright red in color and have no disagreeable odor. Picked lobster meat will be snowy white with red tints, while crab meat is white with red or brown tints, depending on the species or the section of the body it was picked from. Cooked, picked lobster or crab meat should have good color and no disagreeable odor.

Raw shrimp meat should be firm and have a mild odor. The shells of most varieties are translucent with a grayish green, pinkish tan, or light pink tint. The shells should not have blackened edges or black spots. This is a sign of quality loss. Cooked shrimp meat should be firm and have no disagreeable odor. The color of meat should be white with red or pink tints.

When buying whole squid, look for eyes that are clear and full. The skin should be untorn and the meat very firm. The skin of fresh squid is cream-colored with reddish brown spots; as squid ages, the skin turns pinkish.

Handling and Storage

Finfish and shellfish should be handled with care. Both are highly perishable. Storage life depends on how well you take care of it, whether the seafood is a whole fish or a live oyster. Fish bruises easily, so handle carefully. Lift whole fish with two hands and avoid holding by the tail. Pack all seafood products separately or at the top of your grocery bags.

When your seafood purchase arrives home, store it in the coldest part of your refrigerator at a temperature as close to 32 F as possible. The shelf life depends upon the variety of fish and the quality at time of purchase. Be sure to use fish quickly, within one to two days after you buy it. Fish that is not prepackaged should be washed under cold, running water and patted dry with an absorbent paper towel. The fish should then be wrapped in moisture-proof paper or plastic wrap, placed in a heavy plastic bag, or stored in an air-tight, rigid container until ready for cooking. Some varieties of shellfish, however, require different handling and storage guidelines.

Store shrimp, squid, and shucked shellfish in a leak-proof bag, plastic container, or covered jar.

Store live shellfish in a shallow dish covered with damp towels or paper towels. Never put live shellfish in water or in an air-tight container where they could suffocate and die.

Squid and freshly shucked clams have a shelf life of one to two days.

Shrimp and scallops have a shelf life of about two to three days.

Freshly shucked oysters have a shelf life of five to seven days.

Mussels and clams in the shell (live) should be used within two to three days; oysters in the shell, from seven to ten days. Some shells may open during storage. If so, tap them. They will close if alive; if not, discard immediately.

Live lobsters and crabs should be cooked the same day they are purchased. Cooked whole lobsters or crabs should be stored in tight air-tight containers and used within two to three days. Cooked, picked lobster or crab meat should be stored in a sealed moisture-proof plastic bag or air-tight plastic container for three to four days. Pasteurized crab meat can be refrigerated for up to six months before opening and should be used within two to three days after opening.

Refrigerate left-over cooked shellfish dishes as you would any other leftovers. Use within two or three days. Do not allow cooked seafood to come in direct contact with raw seafood or other raw meats.

Frozen Seafood

Purchasing

The technology of handling seafood has improved tremendously in recent years. Today, consumers can find a wide choice of top-quality and wholesome seafood in the freezer case. Commercially frozen fish has been quickly frozen at its peak. When properly thawed, frozen fish is comparable to fish that was never frozen. Yet there are some important points to keep in mind when purchasing and handling frozen seafood. Frozen fish and shellfish should be packaged in a close-fitting, moisture-proof package. Select packages from below the load line of the freezer case. Look for packages that still have their original shape and the wrapping intact with no ice visible. Do not allow the package to defrost during transportation. Frozen prepared shellfish, such as crab cakes or breaded shrimp, clams, or oysters should be frozen solid with no signs of freezer burn such as discoloration or drying on the surface and no objectionable odor.

Storage

After shopping, immediately store commercially wrapped frozen seafood in your freezer. Store frozen seafood in the coldest part of the freezer and hold at 0°F or preferably colder, as close to-20°F as possible. As with other frozen foods, avoid prolonged storage by planning your purchases, keeping in mind first in, first out. Commercially frozen seafood can be stored in the freezer for up to six months. Many fish and shellfish are "flash frozen" within hours of harvest, while it might take several days for the same seafood to make it to your supermarket as "fresh." Keep this in mind when deciding to freeze fish at home. Freezing fish at home should be reserved for those times when you end up with more product than you can immediately eat, such as after a fishing trip or if someone cancels out for dinner. Also, freezing fish or shellfish in the home freezer will not improve quality; it only maintains it, at best.

To freeze seafood at home, start with high quality and carefully handled product. Fish should be cleaned first under cold water and then patted dry. Wrap with plastic wrap, excluding as much air as possible. Then overwrap your fish with freezer paper or aluminum foil. There are also specially designed plastic bags for use in the freezer. These may also be used for fish. Carefully seal all packages and label with contents, amount, and date. Place package in the coldest part of the freezer and where the cold air can circulate around them, freezing them quickly. Shellfish such as shucked clams, oysters, or mussels can be frozen in rigid air-tight plastic containers. Be sure the meats are covered with their liquor and there is 1/2 inch space between the liquid and the container lid to allow for expansion. Scallops may be frozen in plastic freezer bags. Be sure to exclude air and seal tightly or pack scallops tightly in covered freezer containers. Shucked shellfish can be stored for three to four months. Most shrimp available in the market has been previously frozen. Be sure shrimp has not been frozen if you plan to freeze it. Refreezing shrimp under non-commercial conditions can significantly affect the flavor and textures, and, in some cases, may make the shrimp, when thawed, unsafe to eat.

Thawing

It is not always necessary to thaw seafood before cooking, depending on how it will be prepared. If thawing is not necessary, simply double the cooking time. But, if your recipe calls for coating, rolling, or stuffing, or if the fish is in a block, you will need to defrost to facilitate handling. If you plan ahead, defrost the fish overnight in the refrigerator. This is the best way to thaw fish in order to minimize loss of moisture. A one-pound package will defrost within 24 hours. Never defrost seafood at room temperature or with hot or warm water. You will destroy the flesh. If you forget to take your seafood out of the freezer ahead of time, place it in a sink of cold water or under cold, running water. A one-pound package will defrost in approximately one hour. You may also use your microwave oven to partially thaw your fish. Use the lowest defrost setting, which is usually 30% power and follow the manufacturer's instructions for time based on amount of fish. (One pound of fillets defrosts in approximately five-six minutes.) Test; seafood should feel cool, pliable, and slightly icy. Be careful not to overheat and begin the cooking process.

How can you figure out if the fish is fresh?

The fish's eyes should be clear and bulge a little. Only a few fish, such as walleye, have naturally cloudy eyes.

Whole fish and fillets should have firm and shiny flesh. Dull flesh may mean the fish is old. Fresh whole fish also should have bright red gills free from slime.

If the flesh doesn't spring back when pressed, the fish isn't fresh.

There should be no darkening around the edges of the fish or brown or yellowish discoloration.

The fish should smell fresh and mild, not fishy or ammonia-like

Why Seafood Spoils

Spoilage begins as soon as seafood species die. Their normal defense mechanisms stop working and a series of changes begin that cause spoilage. These changes are caused by bacteria, enzymes and chemical action.

Spoilage By Bacteria

Bacteria are the most important cause of seafood spoilage. Millions of bacteria are present in the surface slime, on the gills, and in the gut of living seafood species. When seafood species die, bacteria, or the enzymes they produce, invade the flesh through the gills, along blood vessels, and directly through the skin and belly cavity lining. In the flesh, bacteria grow and multiply, producing compounds which are responsible for "fishy" odors and flavors, and discolorations associated with stale seafood. If food poisoning bacteria are present, they can multiply and cause illness when the seafood is eaten.

Spoilage By Enzymes

Many different enzymes are present in living seafood species. They help build tissue, contract and relax muscles, and digest food. When seafood species die, enzymes continue to work and start to digest or breakdown the flesh. This causes the flesh to soften and lowers the quality. Enzymes also produce more food for bacteria to feed on, increasing the rate of spoilage.

Spoilage By Chemical Action

Oxygen in the air can attack unsaturated oils in seafood causing rancidity, off-odors and off-flavors. This is especially important in fatty fish such as salmon and mackerel.

Slowing Seafood Spoilage

All of the changes that cause seafood spoilage are affected by temperature. High tempera tures speed spoilage and low temperatures slow spoilage. For many seafood species, increasing the temperature from 32F to 40F doubles the rate of spoilage and cuts the shelf life in half.

Sanitation is also important. Contamination of seafood by bacteria from dirty ice, containers and surfaces can increase the number of bacteria on seafood and speed spoilage. Contamination with food poisoning bacteria can cause illness when the seafood is eaten. Keeping seafood handling and storage equipment clean reduces bacterial contamination and slows spoilage.

Shelf Life

The approximate shelf life for fresh fish fillets is:

Holding Temperature (°F)	High Quality Shelf Life	Edible Shell Life
90	14 hours	1 day
60	1½ days	2½ days
42	3 days	6 days
32	8 days	14 days
30	10 days	17 days
29	12 days	20 days

Effect of Temperature on Shelf Life

	Holding Temperature (°F)							

		29		30	32	34	36	38	40	45	50	55	60	65

Time at Holding Temperature	Equivalent Age of Product in Days at 32°F											

2 hours	0.1	0.1	0.1	0.1	0.1	0.1	0.2	0.2	0.3	0.4	0.5	0.7
4 hours	0.1	0.1	0.2	0.2	0.2	0.3	0.3	0.5	0.7	0.9	1.1	1.3
6 hours	0.2	0.2	0.3	0.3	0.4	0.4	0.5	0.7	1.0	1.3	1.6	2.0
12 hours	0.3	0.4	0.5	0.6	0.7	0.9	1.0	1.5	2.0	2.6	3.3	4.0
18 hours	0.5	0.6	0.8	0.9	1.1	1.3	1.6	2.2	3.0	3.9	4.9	6.0
1 day	0.7	0.8	1.0	1.2	1.5	1.8	2.1	3.0	4.0	5.2	6.5	8.0

2 days	1.4	1.6	2.0	2.5	3.0	3.6	4.2	5.9			

3 days	2.1	2.4	3.0	3.7	4.5	5.3	6.3				

4 days	2.8	3.2	4.0	4.9	7.1	8.4					

5 days	3.5	4.0	5.0	6.2								

6 days	4.1	4.7	6.0								

7 days	4.8	5.5	7.0									

8 days		5.5		6.3	8.0							

9 days	6.2	7.1										

10 days	6.9	7.9									

11 days	7.6											

12 days	8.3											

Example			

	Actual Elapsed Time	Temp.	Equivalent Age at 32°F

Fish Caught	2 hours	60°F	0.5 days
Storage on vessel	3 days	34°F	3.7 days
Processing	12 hours	45°F	1.5 days
Distribution	12 hours	36°F	0.7 days
Retail case	1 day	38°F	1.8 days

TOTAL	**5.1 days**		**8.2 days**

Remaining high quality shelf life at		32°F	5 hours

Remaining edible shelf life at		32°F	5.8 days

		40°F	2.7 days

Various Shellfish-Associated Toxins

Shellfish poisoning is caused by a group of toxins elaborated by planktonic algae (dinoflagellates, in most cases) upon which the shellfish feed. The toxins are accumulated and sometimes metabolized by the shellfish. The 20 toxins responsible for paralytic shellfish poisonings (PSP) are all derivatives of saxitoxin. Diarrheic shellfish poisoning (DSP) is presumably caused by a group of high molecular weight polyethers, including okadaic acid, the dinophysis toxins, the pectenotoxins, and yessotoxin. Neurotoxic shellfish poisoning (NSP) is the result of exposure to a group of polyethers called brevetoxins. Amnesic shellfish poisoning (ASP) is caused by the unusual amino acid, domoic acid, as the contaminant of shellfish.

Nature of Acute Disease: Types of Shellfish Poisoning. Paralytic Shellfish Poisoning (PSP) Diarrheic Shellfish Poisoning (DSP) Neurotoxic Shellfish Poisoning (NSP) Amnesic Shellfish Poisoning (ASP)

Nature of Disease: Ingestion of contaminated shellfish results in a wide variety of symptoms, depending upon the toxins(s) present, their concentrations in the shellfish and the amount of contaminated shellfish consumed. In the case of PSP, the effects are predominantly neurological and include tingling, burning, numbness, drowsiness, incoherent speech, and respiratory paralysis. Less well characterized are the symptoms associated with DSP, NSP, and ASP. DSP is primarily observed as a generally mild gastrointestinal disorder, i.e., nausea, vomiting, diarrhea, and abdominal pain accompanied by chills, headache, and fever. Both gastrointestinal and neurological symptoms characterize NSP, including tingling and numbness of lips, tongue, and throat, muscular aches, dizziness, reversal of the sensations of hot and cold, diarrhea, and vomiting. ASP is characterized by gastrointestinal disorders (vomiting, diarrhea, abdominal pain) and neurological problems (confusion, memory loss, disorientation, seizure, coma).

Diagnosis of Human Illness: Diagnosis of shellfish poisoning is based entirely on observed symptomatology and recent dietary history.

Associated Foods: All shellfish (filter-feeding molluscs) are potentially toxic. However, PSP is generally associated with mussels, clams, cockles, and scallops; NSP with shellfish harvested along the Florida coast and the Gulf of Mexico; DSP with mussels, oysters, and scallops, and ASP with mussels. **Relative Frequency of Disease:** Good statistical data on the occurrence and severity of shellfish poisoning are largely unavailable, which undoubtedly reflects the inability to measure the true incidence of the disease. Cases are frequently misdiagnosed and, in general, infrequently reported. Of these toxicoses, the most serious from a public health perspective appears to be PSP. The extreme potency of the PSP toxins has, in the past, resulted in an unusually high mortality rate.

Course of Disease and Complications:

PSP: Symptoms of the disease develop fairly rapidly, within 0.5 to 2 hours after ingestion of the shellfish, depending on the amount of toxin consumed. In severe cases respiratory paralysis is common, and death may occur if respiratory support is not provided. When such support is applied within 12 hours of exposure, recovery usually is complete, with no lasting side effects. In unusual cases, because of the weak hypotensive action of the toxin, death may occur from cardiovascular collapse despite respiratory support.

NSP: Onset of this disease occurs within a few minutes to a few hours; duration is fairly short, from a few hours to several days. Recovery is complete with few after effects; no fatalities have been reported.

DSP: Onset of the disease, depending on the dose of toxin ingested, may be as little as 30 minutes to 2 to 3 hours, with symptoms of the illness lasting as long as 2 to 3 days. Recovery is complete with no after effects; the disease is generally not life threatening.

ASP: The toxicosis is characterized by the onset of gastrointestinal symptoms within 24 hours; neurological symptoms occur within 48 hours. The toxicosis is particularly serious in elderly patients, and includes symptoms reminiscent of Alzheimer's disease. All fatalities to date have involved elderly patients.

Target Populations: All humans are susceptible to shellfish poisoning. Elderly people are apparently predisposed to the severe neurological effects of the ASP toxin. A disproportionate number of PSP cases occur among tourists or others who are not native to the location where the toxic shellfish are harvested. This may be due to disregard for either official quarantines or traditions of safe consumption, both of which tend to protect the local population.

Food Analysis: The mouse bioassay has historically been the most universally applied technique for examining shellfish (especially for PSP); other bioassay procedures have been developed but not generally applied. Unfortunately, the dose-survival times for the DSP toxins in the mouse assay fluctuate considerably and fatty acids interfere with the assay, giving false-positive results; consequently, a suckling mouse assay that has been developed and used for control of DSP measures fluid accumulation after injection of the shellfish extract. In recent years considerable effort has been applied to development of chemical assays to replace these bioassays. As a result a good high performance liquid chromatography (HPLC) procedure has been developed to identify individual PSP toxins (detection limit for saxitoxin = 20 fg/100 g of meats; 0.2 ppm), an excellent HPLC procedure (detection limit for okadaic acid = 400 ng/g; 0.4

ppm), a commercially available immunoassay (detection limit for okadaic acid = 1 fg/100 g of meats; 0.01 ppm) for DSP and a totally satisfactory HPLC procedure for ASP (detection limit for domoic acid = 750 ng/g; 0.75 ppm).

Sushi Terminology

Sushi is defined as food made from rice seasoned with vinegar and served with raw fish. But this is a common misconception the word sushi actually refers to a type of preparation which evolved from an ancient Japanese way of preserving fresh fish, covered with seasoned rice to protect the delicate fish this soon evolved to the familiar style of cuisine that we all know today. There many types of sushi the most recognized styles are:

Nigiri: This type of sushi involves pressing a small amount of rice between your palm to form a shape of small football which then a small amount of wasabi is added and it is top with a piece of raw fish.

Maki/Furumaki: this are the most familiar of them all it is a type of roll that incorporates seasoned rice, Nori (Dried Seaweed) and your choice of fish then its rolled and cut to order.

Temaki: this type of sushi is known as a hand roll because it is typically done by placing a piece of Nori and filling it with toppings then rolling it in you palm hence the name.

Over the years sushi has evolved to incorporate more modern styles of cookery, now you can cook hot food and it can still pass for sushi, so not to be left behind here are a few terms and definitions along with a couple of recipes to boost your understanding of the great art of Sushi.

Aburage-Deep-Fried Tofu Pouches
Aji-Horse Mackerel
Akagai-Ark Shell or Pepitoma Clam
Ama-Ebi-Raw Shrimp
Anago-Sea or Conger Eel
Aoyagi-Round Clam
Awabi-Abalone
Ayu-Sweetfish
Buri-Adult Yellowtail
Chutoro-Marbled Tuna Belly
Ebi-Boiled Shrimp
Hamachi-Young Yellowtail

Hamo-Pike Conger; Sea Eel
Hatahata-Sandfish
Hikari-Mono-Various Kinds of "Shiny" Fish, Such as Mackerel
Himo-"Fringe" Around an Ark Shell
Hirame-Flounder or Halibut
Hokkigai-Surf Clam
Hotategai-Scallop
Ika-Squid
Ikura-Salmon Roe
Inada-Very Young Yellowtail
Kaibashira-Eye of Scallop or Shellfish Valve Muscles
Kaiware-Daikon Radish Sprouts
Kajiki-Swordfish
Kani-Crab
Kanpachi-Lean Yellowtail
Karei-Lean Yellowtail
Katsuo-Bonito Tuna
Kazunoko-Herring Roe
Kohada-Gizzard Shad
Kuruma-Ebi-Prawn
Maguro-Tuna
Makijiki-Blue Marlin
Masu-Trout
Mejia (Maguro)-Young Tuna
Mekajiki-Swordfish
Mirugai-Surf, Geoduck or Horseneck Clam
Negi-Toro-Tuna Belly and Chopped Green Onion
Ni-Ika-Squid Simmered in a Soy-Flavored Stock
Nori-Tama-Sweetened Egg Wrapped in Dried Seaweed
Otoro-Fatty Portion of Tuna Belly
Saba-Mackerel
Sayori-(Springtime) Halfback
Seigo-Young Sea Bass
Shako-Mantis Shrimp
Shima-Aji-Yellow Jack
Shime-Saba-Mackerel (Marinated)
Shiromi-Seasonal "White Meat" Fish
Suzuki-Sea Bass
Tai-Red Snapper

Tairagai-Razor-Shell Clam
Tako-Cooked Octopus
Tamago-Sweet Egg Custard Wrapped in Dried Seaweed
Torigai-Japanese Cockle
Toro-Fatty Tuna Belly
Tsubugai-Japanese Shellfish
Uni-Sea Urchin Roe

Pickled Ginger

Ingredients:
1 C. Peeled Ginger
1 C. Rice Wine Vinegar
1 Tsp. Red Miso
1 Tsp. Honey

Directions:
-soak and cover ginger in water overnight. Mix all other ingredients and bring to a boil and quickly cool. Pack ginger and cooled mixture into 1 pint jar. Heat in water bath.

Ponzu

Ingredients:
5 oz. soy sauce
4 oz. yuzu sauce
2 in. Kelp
8 oz. rice wine vinegar

Directions:
-mix all ingredients evenly and add Kelp, refrigerate for 3 to 5 days.

California Roll

Ingredients:
8 oz. Cooked Sushi Rice
3 oz. Rice Vinegar
6 oz. Crab Meat
1 Tbsp. Cucumber (Julienne)
1 Tbsp. Avocado

1 oz. Mayonnaise
1 ea. Nori

Directions:
-Mix the rice with vinegar and spread evenly over nori, mix mayonnaise with crab meat and turn the nori over. Add the crab mixture, avocado and cucumber. Using a Maki Sui roll the nori make sure not to roll to tight or mixture will spread out.

Ahi Tartar

Ingredients:
8 oz. Ahi
2 oz. Soy Sauce
½ oz. Sesame oil
1 tsp. Sesame seeds
1 tsp. Lemongrass
1 oz. Teriyaki Sauce
1 tsp. Scallions
1 oz. Thai Sweet Chili
TT Salt/Pepper

Directions:
-Finely Dice the Ahi and Set Aside. In a mixing bowl add all the rest of the ingredients and mix thoroughly, add the ahi and let marinade for 30 min.

Stock's The Foundation Of Any Kitchen

Stock's are the foundation on which kitchens run on, this is indicated by the French word for stock: Fond, meaning "Foundation" or "Base". They earned the reputation as a culinary building block because they are the ultimate fundamental. In classical cuisine, the ability to produce a good stock is the most basic of basic skills because so much of the work done in the day to day production that goes on in a kitchen depends solely on the quality of the stock. Good stock's are the foundation of soups, sauces, stews, and braised foods, stock's are flavorful liquids made by simmering bones, vegetables, and aromatics in a liquid. In addition, they may be the flavorful cooking medium for grains, legumes, and vegetables.

Chef's who are trying to reduce the fat content of any dish have learned to substitute stock, either as is or lightly thickened, to reduce the butter or oil that is ordinarily use. The end result is a dish rich in flavor and low in fat content, Stocks are also a fundamental because they provide an excellent way to learn about culinary concepts: Control over cooking speed and time, ratios, developing flavor, and judging a dish's quality. In modern kitchens stocks have lost much of the importance they once had. Today's professional kitchen may not produce the full range of stocks that make up the traditional repertoire of the classic Escoffier kitchen. Some kitchens may even go as far as too not make stocks as part of their daily mise en place. First because the reliance of portion meats have made it unnecessary for caring or producing stocks; second, stocks require time this means the requirement of extra labor which most restaurants today aren't able to provide. Finally, more food today is served without sauces, so their is no need for stocks. Nevertheless, the finest cuisine still depends on soups and sauces based on high-quality stocks. so stock making still remains an essential skill that you should learn early in your training. Stocks and sauces are almost never served by themselves but are components of many other preparations.

A thorough knowledge of how to select ingredients to produce a specific flavor as well as of the techniques required to extract every bit of flavor while producing a clear, high-quality stock applies in a great number of cooking applications. So if you think that stock making is overrated then maybe you should stick to bases, and powders; but for those who are purest and want to provide your establishment with a good stock, here are some guidelines to go by. Firs start by picking the best and freshest ingredients you can find, and gather all the proper equipment needed ie: stock pots, chinoise, ladle, peeler, etc. second, start by preparing your miropoix (50% Onion, 25% Celery, 25% Carrots) and Bouquet Garni or Sachet D'Espiece, Basically the French term for fresh aromatics. Third prepare your bones by washing them and cleaning them (Removing the excess fat), know if your using chicken bones make sure to wash them thoroughly this reduces the impurities in your stock, if your using beef or veal bones make sure that all usable meat is remove from the carcass. Finally before starting your stock make sure to introduce an acid, the acid will break down the connective tissue which will gelatinous the stock. Here is a sample of a simple stock set-up that can be the foundation of your kitchen.

<u>Basic White Stock</u>

Ingredients:
10-12 lb Bones: Chicken, Veal, or Beef

10-12 Qt Cold Water
Mirepoix
1 lb Onion, Chopped
8 oz Carrot, Chopped
8 oz Celery, Chopped
Sachet
1 ea. Bay Leaf
1/4 tsp Thyme
1/4 tsp Peppercorns
6-8 Parsley Stem
2 ea. Whole Cloves

-add all ingredients to stock pot, bring to a boil and reduce to a simmer, skim as needed. Cook for 6hr. To 24hr.

Basic Brown Stock

Ingredients
10 lb beef bones,(2-inch pieces)
10 Qt. Cold water
1 ea. (6-ounce) can tomato paste
6 oz. olive oil
Miropoix
2 c chopped onions
1 c chopped celery
1 c chopped carrots
2 c red wine
Sachet
2 oz. peppercorns
5 ea. garlic cloves
5 ea. bay leaves
1 tsp thyme

-toss bones in olive oil and roast to a golden brown, add to stock pot. Deglaze roasting pans with 1 c. red wine and add the miropoix and roast and add tomato paste. Deglaze one more time with remaining red wine and add to stock, cook for 6hr. To 30 hr.

Roux's

Roux is a classical French ingredient used as a binder it is a mixture of equal parts butter and flour cooked until a uniform paste is formed and all the raw flour is cooked out.

Blonde Roux-Cooked until flour turns pale and light brown, this roux is used for a variety of things which include thickening soups, stew's, stocks, bouillons, broths and sauces.

White Roux-Cooked just until the flour is integrated and mainly used as a thickener and also to flavor and thicken chowders, soups, and sauces.

Brown Roux-Usually made from flour and pan drippings, this roux is mainly used to flavor stew's, soups, bouillons, etc. considered the most flavorful of the roux's.

Black Roux-Roux that has been cooked for a long time usually a dark brown color used mainly to flavor gumbos, jambalayas and a vast of Creole dishes.

APPETIZERS

1—Acapulco Sunrise Dip

Ingredients:
1 can. Refried Beans
½ C. Salsa
8oz. Sour cheese
1 ea. Avocado (Diced)
2 tbsp. lime juice
½ # Shrimp (Devained, Cooked & Diced)
1 ea. Tomato (Diced)
2 oz. Gold Tequila
***Tortilla Chips

Directions:
-in a mixing bowl add the beans, salsa, tomatoes, and shrimp. Set aside. In a blender add avocado, cream cheese and lime juice. Blend smooth. Remove and add to the previous mixture. Serve with tortilla chips

2—Acapulco Seafood Dip

Add 2 oz. cooked crabmeat, saute 4 oz. Diced red bell peppers until tender and add to the mixture. Top with 1 oz. sautéed bay scallops.

3—Calamari Sunrise Dip

Mix 1 oz. White Tequila with 1 oz Lemon Juice, pour over 5 oz. calamari cut into rings, let mixture sit for 5 min. and fold into the dip.

4—Savory Mango Dip

Remove Shrimp From the master recipe and add 2 oz. diced honeydew, ½ c. diced mango, 2 tbsp. minced mint.

5—Artichoke Dip

Ingredients:
2 can. Artichoke Hearts

2 C. Mayonnaise
1 C. Mascarpone Cheese
TT Salt/Pepper

Directions:
-in a food processor add the artichoke heart, mayonnaise and parmesan. Puree. Season to taste and place in the oven and bake at 350F for 10 min.

6—Artichoke Sun Dip

Dice ½ c. sun dried tomatoes and mix with 2 oz. tomato juice then fold into master recipe.

7—Artichoke Puree

Add 3 oz. manufacturing cream, 1 clv. Minced garlic, 2 oz. black olives and puree in blender or food processor.

8—Pineapple Dip

Dice ½ c. pineapple, dice 1 ea. Red onion, and toss with 3 oz. pineapple juice.

9—Orange Mango Dip

Puree 1 c. mango and mix with 1 c. orange segments and 1 oz. orange zest.

10—Asian Beef Skewers

Ingredients:
3 tbsp. Hoisin Sauce
3 tbsp. Sherry
¼ C. Soy Sauce
1 tsp. BBQ Sauce
2 ea. Scallions (Chopped)
2 ea. Garlic (Minced)
1 tsp. Ground Ginger

1 # Flank Steak
*** Skewers

Directions:
-cut the steak into 1 oz. strips and insert the skewers. In a mixing bowl add the rest of the ingredients and pour over the skewers let sit for 5 min. then grill

11—Tropical Pineapple Skewers

Cut 2 in. cubes from ½ pineapple, and arrange in intervals (meat, pineapple, meat), Reduce 1 c. of Coconut milk until syrup consistency and glaze the skewers.

12—Curried Beef Satay

Mix 2 oz. yellow curry with 2 oz. canola oil and pour over the satay, let sit for 2 hrs. before you grill.

13—Blackened Beef Skewers

Drench the beef in 3 oz. Cajun Spice and grill on high heat to get a heavy sear and smoky flavor.

14—Bouchee's Diane

Ingredients:
10 ea. Round Bouches
4 oz. Duck Confit
1 oz. Black Truffle
2 oz. Salmi's Sauce

Directions:
-Combine the duck confit with the truffles and blend smooth. Top the bouches with the mixture and pour over the sauce.

15—Bouchee's Rayne

Remove the Salmi sauce from the master recipe, add a blend in 3 oz. honey and 3 oz. soy sauce.

16—Bouchee's A L' Armoricaine

Toss mixture with 4 oz. tomato sauce, and 2 oz. cooked lobster meat and top with chiffonade Basil.

17—Bouchee Supreme

Dice 1 ea. Avocado, 1 ea. Papaya and toss with 1 oz. minced mint.

18—Corn Salsa

Ingredients:
1 # Corn Kernels
2 oz. lime juice
4 tbsp. olive oil
2 ea. Tomatoes (Diced)
1 C. Black beans (Cooked)
1 ea. Red onion (Diced)
3 tbsp. Parsley (Minced)
2 oz. Cilantro (Minced)
TT Salt/Pepper

Directions:
-in a mixing bowl add all ingredients, mix well and refrigerate for 2 hours. Season to taste and serve with corn chips.

19—Honey Roasted Pineapple Salsa

Cube ½ ea. Pineapple and toss in 6 oz. honey, 8 oz. brown sugar mixture. Spread out on a sheet pan and bake at 350 degrees for 12 to 15 min. cool and puree.

20—Fruit Salsa

Dice 1 ea. Pineapple, 1 ea. Honeydew, 1 ea. Cantaloupe and toss with 1 ea. Minced jalapeno.

21—Kiwi-Peach Salsa

Peel and dice 3 ea. Kiwi, 2 ea. Peaches and mix with 1 tsp. minced mint and 1 ½ oz. Simple Syrup.

22—Crab Stuffed Zucchini

Ingredients:
6 oz. Dungeness Crab
3 ea. Green zucchini
2 ea. eggs, beaten
1 oz. Dijon
1 c shredded cheddar cheese
1/2 C. Panko
2 oz. Scallions
TT Salt/Pepper

Directions:
Cut the tips off the zucchini. Blanch In Boiling water and Shock cold in ice bath. Cut zucchini in half lengthwise, scoop out seeds and drain zucchini shells. Combine crab and remaining ingredients. Scoop into piping bag and pipe into shells and bake on greased baking sheet at 350 degrees for 15 minutes.

23—Fried Zucchini

Batter Zucchini in 3 oz. Buttermilk and roll in 4 oz. Panko, Place in refrigerator for 5 min. and fry at 350°.

24—Braised Stuffed Zucchini

Cut the ends of the zucchini and with a long de-corer scoop out the seeds. Add 2 oz. bay shrimp, 1 oz. cheddar to the mixture and pipe inside the zucchini, know place the ends back on and wrap the zucchini in plastic wrap so that the ends don't fall off. Braise in 4 oz. tomato juice.

25—Baked Provolone & Zucchini

Slice the zucchini into thick juliennes and layer in a casserole dish (zucchini, provolone, zucchini) top with master recipe and bake at 350º for 15 to 20 min.

26—Crostini with Truffle-Lavender Olive Paste

Ingredients:
½ C. Kalamata Olive Paste
1 tsp. white truffle oil
½ tsp. lavender flowers
8 ea. Pc. Ciabatta Bread (Cut into ¼ in. Cubes & Toasted)
TT Salt/Pepper

Directions:
-in a small mixing bowl add the olive paste, truffle oil, lavender, salt, and pepper. Mix well. Put paste into a piping bag with a star tip and pipe on to the Italian bread.

27—Olive Tapanade

Add 3 oz. Kalamata olives, 3 oz. olive oil and add to master recipe, place all ingredients into a food processor and pulse.

28—Fried Olive Puff

In a standard mixer add 3 oz. butter, 1 oz. flour and blend. Once the ingredients are evenly incorporated add the master recipe except for the bread, blend smooth. The mixture should be fluffy with no lumps, scoop out using a spoon or ice cream scoop and place into 350º deep fat fryer until golden brown.

29—Olive Mousse

Whip 1 C. manufacturing cream until stiff, then whip 1 C. egg whites until stiff; add the master recipe to the whipped cream and whisk until evenly incorporated know fold in the egg whites and chill.

30—Olive Paste Marinade

Add 1 tsp. paprika, 1 tsp. parsley, 1 tsp. nutmeg, 3 oz. olive oil and whisk together.

31—Cucumber Chicken Pita Sandwich

Ingredients:
8 oz. Chicken (Cooked & Sliced)
2 ea. Cucumber (Diced)
½ C. Yogurt
½ tsp. Dill Weed
¼ tsp. Mint (Minced)
2 ea. Pita Bread
4 ea. Romaine Leaves
1 ea. Tomato (Diced)
1/3 C. Feta Cheese

Directions:
-combine the yogurt, dill weed, mint, cucumber, and spread it on the pita bread. Add the Romaine, chicken, tomatoes, feta cheese and fold over. Serve cold.

32—Caesar Salad Sandwich

Remove cucumber, yogurt, feta and mint from master recipe and add 4 oz. parmesan cheese, 2 ea. Minced anchovies and 1 ½ oz. Caesar dressing. Toss together and stuff the pita.

33—Mediterranean Sandwich

Slice 4 oz. black olives, julienne 1 ea. Red onion and toss with 1 oz. olive oil.

34—Tropical Chicken Sandwich

Dice ½ C. mango, pineapple and toss with 3 oz. glazed pecans

35—Curried Yogurt Dip

Ingredients:
1 C. Plain Yogurt
1 tsp. Thai Sweet Chili Sauce
2 tsp. Curry Powder
1 tsp. Lemon Juice
1 tsp. sugar
TT Salt/Pepper

Directions:
-Mix all ingredients in Food Processor and blend until smooth. Refrigerate for 20 min. before use.

36—Watermelon Yogurt Dip

Puree 1 C. seedless watermelon and blend into master recipe, remove curry from this recipe. Top with 2 oz. dice watermelon.

37—Cranberry-Passion Fruit Dip

Substitute passion fruit yogurt for the plain yogurt, whisk in ½ c. dried cranberries and 1 oz. simple syrup

38—Chunky Orange Dip

Remove curry and add ½ c. orange segments, 3 oz. orange zest, 2 oz. orange juice and 3 ea. Diced strawberries.

39—Braised Mango Chutney

Dice 2 ea. Mango, and add 1 c. orange juice, 6 oz. sugar, 2 oz. Bourdoux, 2 oz. cornstarch and reduce until thicken.

40—Eggplant Encrusted Parmigiana

INGREDIENTS:
1 c olive oil
1 ea. Eggplant cut into rounds
2 red bell peppers, chopped
1 tbsp. chopped fresh basil
1 tbsp. chopped fresh oregano
2 oz. balsamic
2 oz. red wine
4 oz. Raw sugar
8 slices mozzarella cheese
1 small onion, chopped
2 cloves garlic, minced
1 c. Diced Tomatoes
4 tbsp. tomato paste
4 anchovy fillets, chopped
3 tbsp. capers, chopped
1 c grated Parmesan cheese
TT Salt/Pepper

DIRECTIONS:
Saute eggplant until coated with oil. line the bottom of a casserole dish. Saute the red peppers until tender, and layer over eggplant in casserole dish. Top with mozzarella. Heat and cook onions and garlic until lightly browned and caramelized. Stir in stewed tomatoes, basil, and oregano and simmer 5 minutes. Add balsamic vinegar, red wine vinegar, brown sugar, and tomato paste. Simmer for 10 minutes. Add anchovy filets and capers. Season with salt and pepper. Pour over the mozzarella cheese in the casserole dish. Sprinkle Parmesan cheese on top of sauce. Bake in preheated oven for 35 min, or until cheese is Crispy and golden.

41—Braised Eggplant Napoleon

Layer the eggplant by placing 1 slice provolone and prociutto, place in casserole dish and fill half the way with tomato sauce.

42—Eggplant Ratatouille

Add 2 ea. Jumbo eggplant diced, 1 ea. Diced onion, 1 ea. Diced red bell pepper, 1 tsp. chiffonade basil, 1 tsp. chopped parsley, 1 tbsp. tomato puree.

43—Eggplant Wellington

Add 1 tsp. chopped shallots, 2 tsp. morel mushrooms, saute until paste like consistency and place on 4x4 sheet of puff pastry, add the master recipe, fold close and brush the pastry with egg yolks and bake at 350º for 20 min.

44—Fried Calamari

Ingredients:
1 # Calamari Cut into Rings
6 oz. Flour
1 C. Condense Milk
1 oz. Salt
1 oz. Black Pepper
1 tsp. cayenne
1 tsp. Cumin
1 tsp. Paprika
1 tsp. Dry Thyme
1 tsp. Onion Powder

Directions:
-soak the rings in the milk for about 15 min. then gather all the dry ingredients and mix together. Pre heat deep fat fryer to 375F. Remove the rings from the milk and batter in the flour mixture drop into the fryer for **1 min.** no more or else the rings will become tough.

45—Calamari Stir-Fry

Follow the breading of the master recipe except for the condensed milk, using a hot Wok add ½ c. canola oil, 2 oz. green peas, 2 oz. corn kernels, 3 oz. sliced mushrooms, 1 ea. Julienne red bell peppers and stir fry until tender, add the calamari and stir fry for an additional 2 minutes, finish with soy sauce.

46—Grilled Calamari

Season calamari with salt, pepper, cayenne, cumin and place calamari on 6" skewers; grill over low heat.

47—Calamari Frittata

Mix all ingredients and blend in with 8 ea. Eggs and top with cheddar cheese and parmesan cheese, bake ate 350° for 10 min.

48—Gratin au Chou

INGREDIENTS:
2 garlic cloves, crushed
1 tsp. Thai Sweet Chili
1 oz. butter, melted
4 oz cream
1 Tbsp. Kalamata olive oil
5 oz. bacon, chopped
10 oz. Nappa Cabbage, shredded
1 onion, finely sliced
4 oz. milk
1/4 tsp nutmeg
1-1/3 lbs. potatoes
3/4 cup grated gruyere
TT Salt/Pepper

DIRECTIONS:
Heat the oil in a saucepan. Add the chopped bacon and cook for 2 to 3 minutes, stirring. Add the shredded cabbage, garlic and chili and cook for 3-4 minutes. Brush the gratin dish with the melted butter. Place the cream in a small saucepan, season with nutmeg and heat just until boiling ~ do not let boil. Remove from heat. Layer the potatoes, cabbage mixture, and cheese in the prepared dish. Finish with a potato layer. Top with more cheese. Pour the cream over the mixture. Place in oven and bake for 45 minutes

49—Chicken Au Chou

Dice 2 ea. 8 oz. chicken breast and dust in flour, pan fry and add 1 oz. cognac, flambé and add to master recipe

50—Shrimp Scallop Au Chou

Season the shrimp and scallops, sear to a golden brown and deglaze pan with white wine and add to master recipe

51—Beef Scallopini Au Chou

Pound out 1 # beef chuck to about ¼ of an inch. Dust in flour and pan fry to a golden brown and layer on bottom of dish

52—Homard Tartar

Ingredients:
2 # Lobster(Cooked & Cut Into Quarters)
1 # Shrimp (Cooked)
8 oz. Scallops (Cooked)
4 oz. Garlic (Minced)
1 ea. Shallot (Minced)
3 ea. Scallions
4 oz. Cream Fresh
4 oz. Butter
2 oz. Salt
2 oz. Black Pepper
2 oz. paprika

Directions:
-Add all ingredients into a food processor and lightly pulse until you get half pureed and half chunky it should be an even contrast that holds and gives at the same time.

53—Lobster A L'Americaine

Mix the master recipe with tomato sauce and chopped parsley, and fill small boul au vent top with chiffonade basil

54—Lobster Spaghetti

Dice 1 ea. Onion, slice ½ c. mushrooms and saute, add 1 c. tomato sauce and bring to a simmer, add pre-cooked spaghetti and toss. Finish with chopped parsley

55—Lobster Melt

Place all ingredients into food processor and ground, add 1 oz. balsamic, 1 oz. parsley, 1 oz. soy sauce, 1 oz. molasses, 1 tsp. cinnamon, 1 ½ c. panko and 2 ea. Eggs; mix all ingredients until evenly incorporated, portion out 8 oz. patties and sear over medium heat, top with confit onions

56—Jumbo Garlic Shrimp

Ingredients:
48 ea. Jumbo Shrimp
4 tbsp. cayenne pepper
6 tbsp. Garlic powder
2 C. Olive oil
1 oz. Black Pepper

Directions:
-in a large mixing bowl add all ingredients and mix well, in a saute pan add half the shrimp and saute, remove add the rest and saute.

57—Grilled Jamaican Shrimp

Add all ingredients into mixing bowl and add 3 oz. canola oil, 2 tsp. Jamaican jerk and toss together. Let sit for 10 min. and place shrimp on 6 " Skewers; grill for 45 se. on each side

58—Shrimp Alfredo

Saute the shrimp in 1 oz. brown butter, add 4 c. manufacturing cream and reduce by half, next add 1 c. parmesan and pre-cooked fettuccini and toss, finish with chopped parsley

59—Coconut Shrimp

Prepare flore mixture with coconut shavings at the end, batter the shrimp and let sit for 10 min. deep fry to a golden brown

60—Shrimp and Potato Curry

Peel and bake 3 potatoes, in a sauce pot add 3 oz. curry and 3 c. manufacturing cream, bring to a boil and add 2 ea. Diced carrots, 1 ea. Diced celery and dice the potatoes and add to curry; next add the shrimp and simmer for 10 min.

61—Mushroom Duxelle

INGREDIENTS:
1 lb. mushrooms, coarsely chopped
5-10 shallots, chopped
4 garlic cloves, germ removed, chopped
3 Tablespoons olive oil
OPTIONAL: may use some chopped hard boiled eggs and/or chopped parsley as a garnish

DIRECTIONS:
Heat a large saucepan over med-high heat and pour in the olive oil. Heat the oil. Add the mushrooms, shallots and garlic and cook, stirring once in a while, until browned. Season with salt and continue cooking until the mushrooms have given off their liquid. Continue to cook and stir until the liquid has evaporated. When the mixture is dry, place in a food processor and pulse to form a chunky paste

62—Mushroom Caviar

Mix ½ tsp. sodium alginate with 6 oz. water and mushroom duxelle, in a separate bowl add ½ tsp. calcium chloride and 10 oz. water and let sit until calcium incorporates. Add mushroom mixture to a dropper and slowly pour one drop at a time into the calcium mixture

63—Fried Mushrooms

Toss 1 c. button nose mushrooms in 3 oz. olive oil, 1 tsp. garlic powder, 1 tsp. paprika, 1 tsp. salt, 1 tsp. black pepper and batter in 4 oz. water, 2 oz. flour and 1 oz. cornstarch. Fry at 350°

64—Mushroom and Shallot Bruchetta

Dice 3 oz. crimini, oyster, shitake and morel mushrooms. Mince 3 ea. Shallots and lightly saute all ingredients for 2 min. remove and toss with tomato paste, 1 tsp. parsley, 3 oz. parmesan cheese and season to taste

65—Rabbit Tots

Ingredients:
1 # rabbit meat (ground)
3 ea. Eggs
1 # crushed croutons
1 c. Jalapenos (Diced)
½ C. salt
½ C. onion powder

Directions:
-IN a medium size mixing bowl add all the ingredients and mix until evenly incorporate, form them into 3 oz balls and drop into a 350 degree deep fat fryer until golden brown, remove and place into a 350 degree oven for 10 min. until fork tender.

66—Rabbit Parmesan

Pound 2 ea. Rabbit thighs and prepare flore mixture with 1 c. parmesan added to the panko. Batter and quick sear on both sides and place on a bed of sliced tomatoes and bake at 350° for 7 to 12 min.

67—Lemon Herb Rabbit

Mince 2 tbsp. parsley, thyme, basil and blend together with ½ c. canola oil and 3 oz. lemon juice; truss the rabbit and place inside a casserole dish lined with lemon slices and pour half the marinade and bake at 350° for 30 min. half way threw the cooking process pour the rest of the marinade on top

68—Grilled Rabbit Legs

In a small mixing bowl add 1 tsp. salt, pepper, paprika, cumin, onion powder, garlic powder, brown sugar and whisk until evenly incorporated. Dust the rabbit it the dry rub and grill over low heat until legs are tender

69—Red Bell Pepper Pancakes

Ingredients:
¾ C. Red Roasted Peppers
2/3 C. Flour
1 tbsp. Butter
2 ea. Eggs, Large
¼ C. Cornmeal
3 tbsp. Coriander
1 Pnt. Sour Cream

Directions:
-in a food processor add the bell peppers, sour cream, 1 egg and mix until smooth. Remove and place into a mixing bowl add coriander, cornmeal, flour and egg. Mix until smooth and creamy. In a saute pan add the butter and pour in the mixture. The cakes should be light and fluffy.

70—Red Bell Pepper Sauce

In a food processor add 4 ea. Roasted red bell peppers and puree. Hold for later. In a small sauce pot saute 1 oz. minced shallots and degalze with white wine, add 1 c. chicken stock and reduce by half; add 2 oz. cream and roasted peppers, bring to a simmer and finish with 2 oz. butter

71—Crab Stuffed Peppers

Cut the top of the peppers and remove the seeds, toss in olive oil. For the crab mixture add 1 c. cooked crab meat, 3 oz. shitake mushrooms, ½ c. panko, and 2 oz. mayonnaise. Mix thoroughly and stuff the peppers with the mixture, top with mozzarella and bake at 350º for 15 min.

72—Red Pepper Dip

Add 3 ea. Roasted bell peppers into food processor and puree, add 1 c. cream cheese, 1 tsp. parsley, 1 tsp. cumin and puree for an additional minute, season to taste

73—Saffron Glazed Prawns

Ingredients:
1 C. Pinot Grigio
8 Sprigs. Saffron
2 oz. honey
1 tsp. curry powder
1 tsp. Thyme (Minced)
1 tsp. Parsley (Minced)
1 tsp. Rosemary (Minced)
1 Pc. Garlic (Minced)
3 oz. Butter
1 # Prawns
TT Salt/Pepper

Directions:
-in a medium size saute pan add the pinot grigio and let reduce fro 5 min. then add the honey, curry powder, thyme, parsley, rosemary, garlic, saffron. Cook for

10 min. until it is aromatic and then add the prawns and butter cook for 7 min. and season to taste, they should be bright red when ready.

74—Poached Prawns

In a medium size sauce pot add 1 qrt. Water, 2 c. red wine, 1 oz. black peppercorns, 3 ea. Bay leaf and bring to a boil and reduce to a simmer. Poach prawns until just translucent

75—Shrimp A L'Americaine

Saute 4 oz. tiger shrimp, 4 oz. rock shrimp in brown butter, season to taste. Place inside puff pastry Vol Au Vent top with Chiffonade Basil

76—Prawn Skewers

Arrange 3 prawns on a 6" skewer layered with Maui Onions in between each prawn, season with 1 tsp. cumin, 1 tsp. paprika, salt/pepper and grill over low heat

77—Scallop Fritters

Ingredients:
1 # diver scallops (cleaned & diced)
4 oz. butter
3 c. crumble croutons
2 oz. parsley (chopped)
1 oz. garlic (minced)
2 oz. shallots(Minced)
2 tbsp. balsamic
3 ea. Eggs
2 oz. black pepper
3 oz. salt

Directions:
-In a medium size mixing bowl add all the ingredients and mix well until evenly incorporated, slowly pick up about a hand full and start pressing it between

your palms until you make a firm oblique patty. After they have all been form slowly sear them on a flat top, after they are seared put them into a 350 degree oven for approximately 10 min. or until they are firm to the touch. Can be served with tartar sauce.

78—Horseradish Encrusted Scallops

Mix 3 oz. sour cream with 1 c. panko and 3 oz. horseradish. Encrust both sides of scallops and pan fry to a golden brown

79—Scallop Scampi

Remove eggs from master recipe and replace with 2 oz. diced tomatoes

80—Scallop Popcorn

Bread the scallops in a flore mixture and deep fry at 350° for 2 to 5 min.

81—Fettuccini and Bay Scallops

Saute the scallops in brown butter and add 1 c. manufacturing cream, reduce by 1/3 and add 1 c. parmesan cheese and pre-cook fettuccini, toss and finish with minced parsley

82—Soufflé Au Brocoli

INGREDIENTS:
1 cup Cream
1 thick onion slice
small bay leaf
6 whole black peppercorns
5 Tablespoons butter
2 Tablespoons flour
salt, pepper, grated nutmeg
4 egg yolks
1/3 cup grated Gruyère

1 lb. broccoli florets, cooked in boiling water until tender, and puréed
1 teaspoon Dijon mustard
6 egg whites
butter and 1 Tablespoon of Parmesan cheese for the soufflé dish

DIRECTIONS:
Butter a 1-1/2 quart soufflé dish with 1 tablespoon of the butter and sprinkle with Parmesan. Turn to coat the dish. Make the white sauce: In a saucepan, add the milk, onion, bay leaf and peppercorns and bring it almost to the boiling point. Remove from heat and allow to stand 10 minutes to infuse the flavors. Melt 2 tablespoons of the butter in a medium saucepan and with a flat whisk, stir in the flour. Cook for 2 minutes. Do not allow it to brown. Remove from heat. Strain the milk into the butter/flour mixture, beating constantly. Return to heat. Continue beating until the mixture comes to a boil and thickens. Season highly with the salt, pepper and nutmeg Melt the remaining 2 tablespoons of butter in a saucepan and cook the broccoli purée until it is dry. Place the white sauce over low heat and beat in the egg yolks, one by one. Stir constantly until the sauce thickens slightly and remove from heat. Stir in the broccoli purée and the mustard.

Stiffly whip the egg whites. Add about 1/4 of the egg whites to the warm broccoli mixture and stir to combine thoroughly. Add this mixture back to the remaining egg whites and fold together as lightly as possible. Pour the mixture into the prepared soufflé dish.

Run your thumb around the edge of the mixture, making a groove in it, this will allow the center to rise in a high cap. Bake about 15-20 minutes.

83—Cheese Souffle

Remove broccoli and Dijon from master recipe replace with 1 c. parmesan and 1 c. mascarpone

84—Apple Bacon Souffle

Render down 4 slices of bacon and dice, peel and de-core 2 apples, place in food processor and puree; add the puree and bacon to master recipe

85—Honey Pecan Souffle

Remove florets from master recipe and add 1 c. honey, ½ c. chopped pecans

Soups And Salads

86—Argentinean Lentil Stew

INGREDIENTS:
1 cup Puy lentils
1 quart water
2 ea. Diced Cooked Bacon
1 cube vegetable bouillon
3 medium tomatoes, peeled and diced
1 large onion, diced
1 Diced Red Potato
1 tsp. cumin
1 large clove garlic
1 tablespoon olive oil
1/4 cup barbeque sauce
1/2 teaspoon paprika
salt and pepper to taste

DIRECTIONS:
Place the lentils and water in a large pot, and mix in the vegetable bouillon. Bring to boil, reduce heat to low, and simmer 20 minutes. Stir the tomatoes, onion, carrot, apple, peas, garlic, olive oil, barbeque sauce, and paprika into the pot. Continue to simmer 20 minutes. Season with salt and pepper to serve.

87—Lentil Ham Stew

Dice 2 c. Tasso Ham and add to master recipe, add 1 tsp. chopped parsley and simmer

88—Chicken Lentil Soup

Dice 2 ea. 8 oz. chicken breast, dust in flour and deep fry to a golden brown, add to master recipe and simmer for 20 min. finish with fried wontons

89—Beef Lentil Soup

Cube 1 # beef chuck toss in flour and pan sear to a golden brown and deglaze with 1 c. beef stock and add master recipe

90—Cream of Lentil Soup

Bring soup to a boil and puree using an immersion blender, while that's going slowly add 1 c. manufacturing cream and 3 oz. brown roux

91—Bean and Meat Soup

INGREDIENTS:
2 tablespoons vegetable oil
1/2 pound bacon, chopped
1 teaspoon cumin
1/2 pound sliced deli turkey meat, torn into pieces
1 onion, sliced
1 (14.25 ounce) can tomato puree
1 tablespoon brown sugar
1 teaspoon prepared mustard
1 pinch salt
1 pinch ground black pepper
1 (15 ounce) can kidney beans, drained and rinsed

DIRECTIONS:
Heat the oil in a large pot over medium heat, and cook the bacon, turkey, and onion until bacon is evenly brown and onion is tender. Mix the tomato puree, brown sugar, and mustard into the pot. Season with salt and pepper. Bring to a boil, reduce heat to low, and simmer 30 minutes, stirring occasionally. Mix the kidney beans and cannelloni beans into the soup. Add water to keep the ingredients covered, if needed. Continue to cook, stirring occasionally, until beans are heated through

92—3 Bean Soup

Add 1 c. pinto beans, 1 c. refried beans, and 2 ea. Diced onion; simmer for 30 to 45 min.

93—Bean Chili

Add 2 c. beef stock, 1 # ground beef, 2 tbsp. roasted garlic, simmer for 45 to 1 hr.

94—Bean Bowtie Soup

Add 1 c. refried beans, 2 ea. Diced tomatoes and 2 c. bowtie pasta; simmer until pasta is al dente

95—Berry Soup

INGREDIENTS
1/2 cup barley
6 cups water
1/2 cup white sugar
1 (10 ounce) package frozen raspberries
1/2 cup raisins
1 cup pitted cherries

DIRECTIONS
In a large bowl, soak the barley in the water overnight; do not drain. In a large saucepan over low heat, simmer the barley for one hour. Then add the sugar, raspberries and raisins and simmer for another 30 minutes. Add the cherries and simmer for another 15 minutes, or until the soup becomes relatively thick. Allow to chill in the refrigerator and serve cold

96—Berry Compote

Remove barley from master recipe and add 2 tsp. cornstarch, reduce by half

97—Pineapple Berry Soup

Dice 2 ea. Pineapple and roast at 350° oven for 10 min. add to soup a long with ½ c. pineapple juice

98—Berry Cream Soup

Add 1 c. plain yogurt, 2 c. manufacturing cream and using an immersion blender puree. Simmer over low heat

99—Chicken Soup Au Pistou

INGREDIENTS:
1 tablespoon olive oil
1/2 pound boneless skinless chicken breasts, cut into bite-size pieces
1 onion, finely diced
3 (14.5 ounce) cans chicken broth
1 (14.5 ounce) can whole peeled tomatoes
1 (14 ounce) can great Northern beans, rinsed and drained
2 carrots, sliced
1 large potato, diced
1/4 teaspoon salt
1/4 teaspoon ground black pepper
1 cup frozen green beans
1/4 cup pesto

DIRECTIONS:
Place the olive oil in a large saucepan and heat over medium-high heat until hot. Add chicken; cook and stir about 5 minutes or until chicken is browned. Add onion; cook and stir 2 minutes. Add chicken broth, undrained tomatoes, northern beans, carrots, potato, salt and pepper. Bring to a boil, stirring to break up tomatoes. Reduce heat to low; cover and simmer for 15 minutes, stirring occasionally. Add green beans and cook for 5 minutes or until vegetables are tender. Ladle soup into bowls, top each with 1 teaspoon pesto and sprinkle with parmesan cheese.

100—Pesto Crusted Chicken Soup

Make the pesto and place in mixing bowl, cube 8 oz. chicken breast and rub with pesto. Pan sear until the pesto adheres to the chicken

101—Chicken Cheese Soup

Dust the chicken in flour and sear to a golden brown add master recipe and add 2 c. cheddar cheese, 1 c. parmesan cheese and 1 c. Monterrey Cheese

102—Bacon and Chicken Pesto Soup

Season the bacon with brown sugar and black pepper, bake at 350° for 15 min. cool and dice; add to master recipe

103—Consomme Poullin

Ingredients:
9 C. Chicken Consomme
1 tbsp. Chicken Breast (Cooked & Julienne)
2 tbsp. Pates D'Italie
½ tsp. Parmesan

Directions:
-heat the consomme and garnish with chicken breast, pates D'italie and a side of Parmesan.

104—Beef Consomme

Add 8 oz. ground beef and follow master recipe; garnish with poached beef brunoise

105—Haitian Consomme

Add 1 c. fresh orange juice, 2 ea. Cloves and garnish with orange supreme

106—Consomme Oeufs

Garnish with sliced hard boil egg

107—Apple Consomme

Add 1 c. apple juice and reduce, garnish with poached julienne apples

108—French Tomato Soup

INGREDIENTS
1 tablespoon butter
1 large onion, chopped
6 tomatoes, peeled and quartered
1 large potato, peeled and quartered
6 cups water
1 bay leaf
1 clove garlic, pressed
1 teaspoon salt
1/2 cup long-grain rice

DIRECTIONS
Melt butter in a large saucepan over medium heat. Saute onions in butter until tender and lightly browned, about 10 minutes. Add tomatoes, and continue cooking for 10 more minutes, stirring frequently. Add the potato, and 2 cups of water. Season with the bay leaf, garlic and salt. Bring to a boil, then reduce heat and simmer, covered, for about 20 minutes. Stir in the remaining water, and bring to a boil again. Discard bay leaf, and strain the solids from the broth, reserving both. Puree the vegetables in a food processor or blender, and stir them back into the broth. Bring to a boil, and add the rice. Cover and simmer over low heat for about 15 minutes, or until rice is tender. Serve hot

109—Tomato Noodle Soup

Add 1 oz. tomato paste and 8 oz. linguini noodles cut into 1" segments, simmer for 20 min.

110—Chicken Tomato Soup

Dice 1 # chicken breast and dust in flour, sear to a golden brown and add to master recipe, simmer for 20 min.

111—Wild Mushroom Tomato Soup

Saute 2 oz. morel mushrooms, 2 oz. oyster mushrooms, 2 oz. hen of the wood mushrooms and add to master recipe

112—Poblano Chile Pepper Soup

INGREDIENTS
6 poblano peppers
2 cups chicken broth
salt and pepper to taste
1/2 teaspoon ground nutmeg
2 cups milk
3 tablespoons margarine
1 tablespoon all-purpose flour

DIRECTIONS
Preheat oven to broil. Place poblano chile peppers on a cookie sheet and place in oven. Allow skin to blacken and blister, turning the chile peppers until all sides are done. (Note: Do not overcook.) When they are done, place them in a paper bag and seal. In about 15 to 20 minutes, take them out of the bag and peel the skin off each one under running water. Remove the stems and seeds. In a blender, combine the chile peppers, broth, salt and pepper to taste and nutmeg. Blend until smooth. In a small saucepan over medium heat, warm the milk and set aside. In another saucepan over medium heat, melt the butter or margarine, add the flour and stir well. Add the warmed milk and stir until well blended. Add the chile pepper mixture and mix well. Reduce heat to low and simmer for 30 minutes.

113—Poblano Avocado Dip

Puree the master recipe and add 3 ea. Diced avocado and 1 oz. sour cream

114—Beef Scallopini and Poblano Soup

Pound 1 # of skirt steak and dust in flour, season heavily with salt and pepper, sear for 3 min. on each side and cut into 1" strips and add to master recipe

115—Stuffed Chile Relleno

Render 1 # bacon and cut into bit size pieces, cube 2 c. fresh mozzarella and mix with bacon, hold for later. Whisk 1 c. egg whites to a stiff peak and hold.

Whisk ½ c. egg yolks to a full bloom and fold in with egg white. Stuff the peppers with mixture and batter in egg batter. Fry at 350°

116—Apple Bacon Tomato Soup

INGREDIENTS:
5 slices bacon
1 tablespoon olive oil
1/2 white onion, chopped
2 teaspoons garlic, minced
2 cups beef stock
1 (15.5 ounce) can pinto beans
1 (14.5 ounce) can Italian-style stewed tomatoes
2 stalks celery, chopped
1 bay leaf
1 medium apple, thinly sliced
1/2 cup red wine
salt and pepper to taste

DIRECTIONS:
Place bacon in a large, deep skillet. Cook over medium high heat until evenly brown. Drain, coarsely chop, and set aside. Heat olive oil in a large saucepan over medium heat, and saute white onion and garlic 3 to 5 minutes, or until tender. Stir in beef stock, pinto beans, tomatoes, celery, and bay leaf. Bring the mixture to a boil. Reduce heat, and simmer. In a small saucepan over medium heat, cook and stir the apple in the red wine until soft. Mix bacon, apple, and remaining red wine into the soup mixture. Season with salt and pepper. Continue to simmer, stirring occasionally until well blended

117—Honey Baked Apple Tomato Soup

Quarter 4 apples and toss in 1 c. honey, 4 oz. brown sugar, 1 oz. cumin and paprika; bake at 350° for 15 min. add to master recipe

118—Roasted Tomato and Apple Stew

Cut 4 ea. Tomatoes, 3 ea. Apples into 2" cubes, toss in olive oil and roast for 20 min. add to master recipe and finish with 2 tbsp. tomato paste

<u>119—Chicken Tomato Stew</u>

Cut 2 ea. Chicken breast into cubes, dust in flour and sear to a golden brown. Add to master recipe and add 1 c. tomato juice and 2 oz. paprika

<u>120—German Leek and Potato Soup</u>

INGREDIENTS
1 cup chopped onion
1/2 cup butter
1 cup chopped leeks
8 potatoes, peeled and sliced
6 cups water
1/2 teaspoon fresh thyme
1 ham bone
1 cup heavy cream
salt and pepper to taste

DIRECTIONS
In a large pot over medium heat, cook onions in butter until translucent. Stir in leeks, potatoes, water, thyme and the ham bone. Bring to a boil, then reduce heat, cover and simmer until potatoes are tender, 20 to 30 minutes. Remove ham bone and puree soup with a blender or food processor. Return to pot, stir in cream, salt and pepper, heat through and serve.

<u>121—Braised Leek Stew</u>

Braise 2 # leeks in 1 G. chicken stock, 4 oz. cornstarch, 1 ea. Minced onion, reduce until paste like consistency add master recipe and finish with 2 tbsp. minced parsley

<u>122—Beef Leek Stew</u>

Cut 2 # beef chuck into 2" cubes, dust in cornstarch and sear to a golden brown add 3 oz. butter and add to master recipe

123—Fried Leek and Potato Stew

Julienne 1 # leeks, dust in flour and deep fry at 350° to a golden brown add to
master recipe

124—Jamaican Spinach Soup

INGREDIENTS
3 tablespoons olive oil
1 onion, chopped
2 stalks celery, chopped
4 cloves garlic, minced
2 tablespoons fresh ginger root, minced
1 tablespoon turbinado sugar
2 teaspoons sea salt
1/4 teaspoon ground turmeric
1/4 teaspoon ground allspice
1/4 teaspoon ground nutmeg
2 potatoes, peeled and diced
4 cups chopped zucchini
6 cups vegetable stock
1 pinch cayenne pepper
1 cup chopped fresh spinach
1/2 red bell pepper, minced

DIRECTIONS
Heat the oil in a large pot over medium heat. Stir in onion, celery, garlic, ginger,
and sugar. Cook 5 minutes, until onion is tender. Season with salt, turmeric,
allspice, and nutmeg. Mix in potatoes and zucchini, and pour in the vegetable
stock. Bring to a boil, reduce heat to low, and simmer 10 minutes, or until potatoes are tender. Remove soup from heat, season with cayenne pepper, and stir
in spinach. Using a hand blender, blend soup until smooth. Garnish with red
bell pepper to serve

125—Cream of Spinach Soup

Blanch 3 c. of spinach and cool in ice bath, add spinach to master recipe and
emulsify with 1 c. cream and reduce by 1/3

126—Jamaican Jerk Chicken Soup

Dice 1 # chicken breast and season heavily with jerk seasoning, grill over low heat and add to master recipe, finish with fried onions

127—Grilled Chicken and Pineapple Soup

Dice 1 ea. Pineapple and 1 # chicken breast, season to taste and grill over low heat; add to master recipe and finish with fried wontons strips

128—Toscana Soup

Ingredients:
5 ½ C. Chicken Stock
½ C. Heavy Cream
2 ea. Russet Potatoes (Diced)
4 C. spinach (Chopped)
1 tsp. red pepper flakes
TT Salt/Pepper

Directions:
-in a sauce pot add the potatoes and lightly saute, add the chicke stock and bring to a simmer, add the spinach, red pepper flakes. Cook for 10 min. then add he cream and season to taste.

129—Chicken Florentine Soup

Dice 1 # chicken breast and pour ½ c. egg whites over it. Dust in flour and deep fry at 350° for 5 min.

130—Chicken and Beef Stew

Cube 2 ea. Chicken breast, 1 # beef chuck and brown, deglaze with 1 c. red wine

131—Chicken Fussily Soup

Dice 3 ea. Chicken breast and sear to a golden brown, add 1 c. diced onions and saute, add master recipe and fussily, stew for 15 min.

132—Asian Spinach Salad

Ingredients:
2 tbsp. fresh orange juice
1 tbsp. rice vinegar
½ ea. Medium jalapeno (Chopped)
1 tbsp. Ginger Root (Grated)
2 Clvs. Garlic (Chopped)
1 tsp. Orange Zest
4 oz. Dried Rice Noodles
4 C. Thorne Spinach
¾ C. Dried Tart Cherry's
1/3 C. Mint (Chopped)
1 ea. Small Cucumber (Sliced)
1/3 C. peanuts
2 oz. Carrots (Shaved)
TT Salt/Pepper

Directions:
-for the dressing stir together the orange juice, rice vinegar, ginger root, garlic, mint, jalapeno, orange zest, pepper. Cook the rice noodles in boiling water for 10 min. remove and drain toss with the spinach, peanuts, cucumber, carrots, cherry's and drizzle the dressing on top.

133—Grilled Pacific Salad

Rub 1 tsp. miso over 8 oz. chicken breast, grill over low heat and drizzle teriyaki sauce over master recipe

134—Candied Citrus and Spinach Salad

Toss 1 tsp. lime zest, 1 tsp. orange zest in 2 oz. sugar and place on sheet pan; bake at 350º for 7 to 10 min.

135—Orange Supreme Florentine

Cut supremes from 2 ea. Oranges and take 1 c. orange juice, 2 oz. cornstarch and cook until thicken, chill and toss with orange supremes

136—Caribbean Waldorf Salad With Golden Raisin Vinaigrette

Ingredients:
1 ea. Half avocado
3 tsp. black raisins,
2 tsp.. spiced pecans
5 oz. mix greens
1 tsp. diced cantaloupe
1 tsp. diced honeydew
1 tsp. diced mango
1 tsp. minced cilantro
Vinaigrette:
3 oz. Golden Raisins
1 tsp. roasted garlic
1 tsp. roasted shallot
1 tsp. Dijon
3 oz. red wine vinegar
3 oz. pineapple juice
2 oz. Malibu coco rum
3 oz. sugar

Directions :
In a blender add all the ingredients for the vinaigrette and blend until smooth and all ingredients bind with each other, in a medium size mixing bowl add the raisins, cantaloupe, honeydew, mango, cilantro and season to taste with salt and pepper, now add the spiced pecans and toss with the mix greens, for the avocado season it well with salt and pepper and place on a very hot grill and grill until soft, place the salad in the center of the plate, drizzle the vinaigrette over salad and top with grilled avocado.

137—Grilled Tropical Fruit Salad

Place fruit on 6" skewer, brush with honey and grill over low heat, top with minced mint

138—Grilled Shrimp and Mango Salad

Dice ½ c. mango and toss with 5 ea. Tiger shrimp, season with 1 tsp. paprika, 1 tsp. cumin, salt and pepper. Grill over low heat

139—Grilled Beef and Tropical Salad

Pound 8 oz. skirt steak and marinade in 1 c. canola oil, 1 tsp. parsley, cinnamon, coriander, paprika, cumin, garlic and let sit for 10 min. grill over low heat

140—Shitake Mushroom-Hazelnut Salad

Ingredients:
4 tbsp. Truffle Oil
1 tbsp. red wine vinegar
1 tbsp. Marjoram(chopped)
¼ Tsp. Honey
TT salt/Pepper
4 oz. Shitake Mushrooms (Sliced & Cooked)
8 C. Mix Greens
¼ C. Hazelnuts (Toasted & Chopped)

Directions:
-In a small mixing bowl ad the first 5 ingredients and whisk together to make the vinaigrette, in another bowl add the mushrooms, greens,and hazelnuts. Toss gently and arrange on a clear plate drizzle the top with the vinaigrette.

141—Grilled Portabella and Beef Salad

Quarter 2 ea. Portabella, and cut 2" cubes of beef chuck and arrange on 6" skewers. Season heavily with olive oil, salt and pepper. Grill over medium heat

142—Chicken Popcorn Hazelnut Salad

Cut 8 oz. chicken breast into 2" cubes, pour 2 oz. egg whites and mix thoroughly. Dust in flour and fry at 350°

143—Duck Mushroom Salad

Score the duck breast on the skin side and sear to a golden brown, saute 1 oz. shitake mushrooms, ½ oz. morel mushrooms, and ½ oz. Oyster mushrooms. Slice the duck breast on a bias and top with sautéed mushrooms

144—Steak And Wild Rice Salad

Ingredients:
8 oz. Flank Iron Steak (Grilled)
3 C. Dirty Wild Rice (Cooked)
½ C. Haricot Verts (Minced)
1 C. Artichoke Hearts (Cut In Half)
½ C. Red Roasted Bell Pepper (Cut In To Cubes)
1 tbsp. Lemon Zest
TT Salt/Pepper
2 Ea. Romaine Leafs

Directions:
-In a Medium mixing bowl add all the ingredients except the steak and romaine leafs, toss together, on a plate add the two romaine leafs and layer the rice mixture on top and the steak on top of the mixture.

145—Chicken and Wild Rice Salad

Pound 8 oz. chicken breast, season with salt and pepper, grill over low heat and brush with teriyaki glaze

146—Pan Fried Shrimp and Wild Rice Salad

Dust 6 ea. Jumbo shrimp in flour and sear over high heat, deglaze with white wine and add chopped shallots, diced tomato and 4 oz. butter

<u>147—Grilled Scallops and Fennel Salad</u>

Remove rice from master recipe and plate. Arrange scallops and fennel on 6"
skewers and grill over low heat and brush with molasses

Sauces

148—Beurruge Sauce

Ingredients:
16 oz. cabernet sauvignon
1 ea. Bay leaf
1 oz. black pepper corns
1 oz. parsley
1 oz. rosemary
1 oz. thyme
1 pc. Shallot (minced)
1 ea. Garlic (Minced)
4 oz. heavy cream
8 oz. butter
TT Salt

Directions:
-in a saucepot add the shallots, bay leaf, peppercorns, parsley, rosemary, thyme, garlic, and cabernet. Cook until it reduces by half, add the cream and reduce again. Mount with butter, season to taste and strain.

149—3 Berry Sauce

Add 2 oz. cranberries, 2 oz. blueberries, 2 oz. raspberries and 1 oz. simple syrup

150—Demi-Bordeaux Sauce

Add 2 c. Bordeaux and reduce by half, add beef demi-glaze and reduce to nape consistency, finish with chopped parsley

151—Roasted Garlic Rouge Sauce

Add 1 c. chicken stock and reduce by half, add 4 oz. roasted garlic and whisk until evenly incorporated, add master recipe

152—Cranberry Rouge Sauce

Add 1 c. cranberry puree and cook for 5 min. add 1 oz. whole cranberries

153—3 Basil Pesto

Ingredients:

1. C Pine Nuts
1 C. Sweet Basil
1 C. Thai Basil
1 C. Greek Basil
1 ½ C. Olive oil
TT Salt/Pepper

Directions:

Toast the pine nuts and put in blender, add the Basils and turn the blender on, slowly start poring the olive oil until the pesto becomes somewhat smooth, season to taste.

154—Creamy Pesto Sauce

Add 1 c. manufacturing cream and reduce by 1/3 and finish with 2 oz. butter

155—Parmesan Cheese Pesto

Cook pesto over low heat whisking constantly, add 1 c. parmesan cheese

156—Roasted Fennel Pesto

Quarter fennel bulbs and toss in olive oil and season with salt and pepper. Roast at 350º for 30 min. puree

157—Cream Cheese Pesto Dip

Add 1 c. cream cheese to standard mixer and whip till soft, add 1 tsp. chopped scallions and slowly add master recipe

158—Amaretto Sauce

Ingredients:
1 C. Ricotta Cheese
1 C. Cream Cheese
½ C. Sugar
¼ C. Amaretto
2 tbsp. Whipped Cream

Directions:
-in a mixing bowl add the cheeses, and sugar blend until smooth add the amaretto and blend together add the whipped cream and blend until smooth.

159—Hazelnut Amaretto Sauce

Toss 1 c. hazelnut in simple syrup, roast at 350° for 15 min. add to master recipe and finish with fresh mint

160—Orange Amaretto Sauce

Reduce 1 c. orange juice by ¼, add 1 tsp. orange zest and add to master recipe and finish with orange supremes

161—Mango Amaretto Sauce

Reduce 2 c. simple syrup by 1/3 and in a separate pan saute 1 c. diced mango in brown butter and sugar.

162—Roasted Pineapple Amaretto Sauce

Cut 1 pineapple into 2" cubes, toss in sugar and roast at 350° for 20 min. add to master recipe

163—Sauce Supreme

Ingredients:
1 C. Chicken Veloute
2 oz. heavy cream
1 oz. Butter
TT Salt/Pepper

Directions:
-in a sauce pot add the chicken veloute and reduce by half add the cream, mount with butter and season to taste.

164—Curry Cream Supreme Sauce

Add 4 oz. curry and cook to a simmer. Finish with 1 tsp. coriander

165—Watermelon Cream Sauce

Add 2 c. pineapple and puree using an emersion blender to a smooth consistency

166—Dijon Bacon Sauce

Render 4 oz. apple wood bacon, add to master recipe and finish with 2 oz. dijon

167—Brandied Raspberry Sauce

Ingredients:
4 oz. Brandy
3 tbsp. Butter
1 oz. Cream
3 oz. Sugar
1 C. Raspberries

Directions:
-in a blender add the raspberries and brandy and blend until smooth. Add to a sauce pot and bring to a boil then reduce to a simmer, add sugar and cream. Cook for 3 min. then add the butter. The sauce should be silky

168—Roasted Garlic Brandy Sauce

Remove raspberries from master recipe and add 4 oz. roasted garlic. Finish with 1 tsp. chopped parsley

169—Cherry Brandy Sauce

Remove raspberries from master recipe, saute 1 c. cherries in 2 tsp. butter and 1 oz. brown sugar

170—Caramelized Onion Sauce

Julienne 1 ea. Onion and saute in 1 tsp. brown butter until onions are caramelized. Add master recipe except for berries

171—Brown Sugar Rum Sauce

Ingredients:
2 ea. Egg yolks
½ C. Brown Sugar
1 C. Cream
3 tbsp. Rum
1 tsp. Nutmeg
4 oz. Butter

Directions:
-in a sauce pot add the brown sugar, butter, and cream whisk until smooth. Add the rum and nutmeg continue to whisk. Whisk in the egg yolks and keep whisking until thicken be careful not to cook the egg.

172—Caramel Rum Sauce

Add 4 oz. simple syrup and reduce by 1/3 add 1 c. caramel

173—Cherry Rum Sauce

Saute 1 c. cherries and deglaze with 1 oz. red wine. Add 1 tsp. minced shallots

174—Pearl Onion Rum Sauce

Peel 4 ea. Pearl onion and saute in brown butter and cook until onions are caramelized

175—Dried Sherry Vinegar

Ingredients:
1 C. Dried Tart Cherries
½ C. Cherry Puree
2 C. White wine vinegar

Directions:
-In a sauce pot add all ingredients and bring to a boil, as soon as it boils remove from heat and place into a non reactive container, let sit in the refrigerator fro 2 days.

176—Roasted Garlic Vinegar

Add 4 oz. roasted garlic to master recipe and blend until smooth. Strain

177—Lemon Sherry Vinegar

Add 3 oz. lemon juice and 1 tsp. lemon zest. Let sit for 30 min.

178—Basil Berry Vinegar

Add 6 oz. sweet basil to master recipe and blend until smooth. strain

179—Ginger Lime Beurre Blanc

Ingredients:
¼ C. white wine
1 ea. Lime juice
3 tsp. ginger
1 ea. Shallot (Minced)
½ # Butter
TT Salt/Pepper

Directions:

-in a sauce pan add the ginger and shallots, saute. Add the white wine, lime juice and reduce. Mount with butter and season to taste.

180—Rosemary Lemongrass Beurre Blanc

Add 1 oz. rosemary and 2 tsp. lemongrass zest

181—Curry Lime Beurre Blanc

Add 1 tsp. curry, 1 oz. cream and whisk smooth

182—Orange Supreme Beurre Blanc

Reduce 1 c. orange juice by half, and finish with 2 oz. orange supremes

183—Honey Basil Beurre Blanc

Add 4 oz. honey to master recipe and finish with chiffonade basil

184—Passion Fruit Blanc

Add ½ c. passion fruit puree and 4 oz. cream, reduce by 1/3

185—Mango A La Vin Sauce

Ingredients:

1 C. Fresh Mango (Small Diced)
4 oz. Simple Syrup
2 oz. Sugar
4 oz. Chardonnay
1 oz. Heavy Cream
1 oz. Butter

Directions:

-in a sauce pot add the mango simple syrup, sugar and chardonnay. Reduce. Add cream and mount with butter.

186—Kiwi Chardonnay Sauce

Dice 1 c. kiwi and saute to a pulp, add master recipe and whisk smooth

187—Star Fruit Vin Sauce

Slice 2 ea. Star fruit and toss in sugar, bake at 350º for 15 min. add to master recipe

188—Saffron Vin Blanc

Add 4 sprigs saffron and whisk until color from saffron bleeds out

189—Red Wine Gastrique

Ingredients:
2 C. Water
4 C. Sugar
2 C. Red Wine
1 Tsp. Black Pepper Corns (Crushed)

Directions:
-in a sauce pot add the water and sugar cook until you get simple syrup 15 min. in another sauce pot add the red wine and black pepper cook until almost boiling. Know in a mixing bowl slowly start to add the simple syrup and red wine start whisking continuously while whisking place bowl in an ice bath whisk until cool. Should be somewhat silky but still thick

190—Cinnamon Gastrique

Melt 2 oz. butter and mix with 1 oz. cinnamon, whisk into master recipe

191—Honey Red Wine Gastrique

Place master recipe in blender and add 1 tsp. nutmeg and 6 oz. honey, blend smooth

192—Lemon Lime Gastrique

Mix 3 oz. lemon and 2 oz. lime juice, add 1 tsp. of lime and lemon zest and slowly add to master recipe

193—Sauce Aurore

Ingredients:
3 C. Veloute
1 C. Tomato Paste
3 oz. Butter

Directions:
-In a sauce pot add the veloute and heat. Add the paste and whisk until evenly incorporated, mount with butter

194—Sauce Provance

Add 2 oz. herb d' Provance and whisk smooth, finish with 1 oz. lime juice

195—Concasse Aurore Sauce

Add 4 oz. concasse tomatoes and 1 tsp. chiffonade basil

196—Lavender Horseradish Sauce

Saute 1 oz. horseradish root, add 1tsp. Lavender and add to master recipe

197—Valrhona Aurore Sauce

Add 1 oz. cream and 2 oz. Valrhona chocolate chunks and whisk smooth

198—Sauce Maltaise

Ingredient:
2 C. Hollandaise
2 oz. Blood Orange Juice
1 tsp. Orange Zest

Directions:
-in a mixing bowl add the Hollandaise, orange juice and zest, whisk until smooth

199—Demi Maltaise Sauce

Add 3 c. beef stock and reduce by ¾, finish with 2 oz. butter

200—Grapefruit Dijon Sauce

Add 4 oz. grapefruit and bring to a simmer, add 1 tbsp. Dijon and finish with 1 tbsp. butter

201—Blueberry Maltaise

Add 4 oz. blueberries into food processor and puree, mix with 4 oz. whole blueberries and add to master recipe

202—Sicilian Ragú

INGREDIENTS:
1/2 # ground beef
1 onion, finely sliced
6 oz. Diced Tomatoes
1 tbsp. tomato paste
1/2 c. well aged dry red wine
2 ea. Vela shanks
1 tsp. parsley
1 tsp. sweet basil
1 tsp. sugar

3 bay leaves
1/2 # peas
1/2 tsp. butter
3 oz. olive oil

DIRECTIONS:
Sauté the veal shank until the meat is done, and set it aside. Brown the ground meat. In a large pot, sauté the onion and the parsley; when the onion has browned lightly add the tomatoes, tomato paste, wine, bay leaves, and basil. Cook the mixture for about 20 minutes. Add the ground beef, season with salt and pepper to taste, and add enough water to cover the ground beef (the bone will likely stick up). Cover and simmer, adding the peas after an 1 1/2 hours, together with the sugar. Replace the cover and simmer for another half hour. Remove the bone, and use the beef in the tripe.

203—Spanish Ragu

Saute 1 # chorizo to a golden brown add master recipe and 1 tsp. saffron. Stew for 15 min.

204—Seafood Ragu

Saute 8 oz. ground tilapia to a golden brown, add 6 oz. dice mahi, 6 oz. diced swordfish, 1 # shrimp, cook for 5 min. and add master recipe

205—Beef Ragu

Dice 1 # beef chuck, dust in flour and sear to a golden brown. Add master recipe

206—Sun Dried Cherry Pinot Noir Sauce

Ingredients:
1 C. sun dried cherry's
½ C. Orange juice
3 oz. port wine
1 tbsp. shallot (minced)

2 C. Chicken Stock
1 C. Pinot Noir
1 tsp. Hoisin sauce
4 oz. butter

Directions:
-in a small mixing bowl add the cherry's, orange juice, port wine, hoisin sauce. In a sauce pot add the shallots, chicken stock, pinot noir and reduce, add the orange juice and cherry's. reduce to au sec. mount with butter.

207—Braised Leek Pinot Sauce

Quarter 1 ½ fennel bulbs and braise in 3 c. chicken stock and 1 tsp. chopped shallots

208—Fried Capper Pinot Sauce

Drain 1 c. cappers, dust in flour and fry at 350° for 3 min.

209—Sun Dried Tomato Bordeaux Sauce

Substitute 1 c. Bordeaux for pinot noir, julienne 6 oz. sun dried tomato and saute in brown butter. Add master recipe

210—Ver-jus Caramel

Ingredients:
1 C. Gold Verjus
3 # Sugar
1 C. Manufactured Cream
2 oz. Raisins (crushed)
3 Oz. Butter

Directions:
-In a medium size sauce pot add the verjus, sugar, and raisins. Let it cook for about 45 min. or until all the liquid has evaporated and the sugar is bloomed, slowly whisk in the butter and the cream until the the caramel becomes smooth

and has a creamy texture. Remove the pot from the heat and let cool, place the pot in an ice bath to speed up the cooling process, the verjus caramel is ready for use.

211—Roasted Shallot and Champagne

Toss 3 ea. Shallots in olive oil, season with salt and pepper roast at 350° for 20 min. add shallots to mixing bowl and emulsify using an emersion blender. Slowly add 1c. Champagne

212—Cherry Caramel Sauce

Flash fry 1 c. cherries in deep fat fryer for 30 sec. add to master recipe

213—Pomelo Kiwi Sauce

Reduce 1 c. pomelo juice by 1/3 add to master recipe and finish with 4 oz. diced kiwi

214—Yakisoba Sauce

Ingredients:
1 #5 can. Oyster Sauce
1 Btl. Kagone Yakisoba Sauce

Directions:
-in a mixing bowl add the two ingredients and mix well

215—Yakisoba Glaze

Add 1 c. teriyaki sauce and reduce to syrup consistency

216—Spicy Soba Sauce

Add 4 oz. soy sauce, 1 oz. chili flakes, 3 oz. Thai chili paste, 1 tsp. scallions and bring to a simmer

217—Honey Ginger Soba Sauce

Saute 2 oz. minced ginger, add master recipe ad finish with 6 oz. honey. Whisk until evenly incorporated

ENTRÉE'S

218—Apple Glazed Pork Roast

Ingredients:
3 # Pork Tenderloin
2 Tbsp. flour
1 Tbsp. fennel; seeds
TT Salt/Pepper
2 C applesauce
2 C brown sugar

Directions:
Mix salt, pepper, fennel seed, and flour together and rub onto
The pork tenderloin. Set on counter for 30 minutes. Place in a 350 degree
oven for 1 hour. Whisk applesauce and brown sugar Then
pour over the roast. Continue baking for an additional 45 min.

219—Cashew Crusted Pork Roast

Crumble 1 c. cashew and place on a sheet pan, drizzle olive oil over the roast
and roll in crumble cashews. Sear and roast

220—Honey Glazed Pork Roast

Mix 1 c. honey with 4 oz. teriyaki sauce and brush the roast every 5 min.

221—Stuffed Pork Roast

Dice ½ loaf sourdough bread and toss with 1 c. chicken stock, 4 oz. parmesan,
1 tsp. paprika, 1 tsp. cumin, salt and pepper. Cut 1" slit at the end of the roast
and run a honing stick threw making a strait whole. Add stuffing to piping bag
and pip inside roast.

222—Asian Mint Pork Tenderloin

INGREDIENTS:
2 pound pork tenderloin
1/3 cup molasses

1/4 cup fresh spearmint, minced
3 tablespoons soy sauce
3 tablespoons hoisin sauce
2 tablespoons water
1 tablespoon fresh ginger, peeled and minced
2 cloves garlic minced
vegetable oil

DIRECTIONS:
Combine everything except the tenderloin and the vegetable oil. Mix well. Place tenderloin in a large resealable bag. Pour marinade over top. Turn to coat. Refrigerator for 8 hours. Preheat grill and coat grates in vegetable oil. Remove tenderloins from marinade and place on grill over medium high heat. Grill for 20 minutes, turning occasionally. Baste with mariande after 10 minutes then discard remaining mariande. Remove from grill when done, let sit for 5 minutes, then carve into thin slices.

223—Pepper Crusted Pork Loin

Crush 6 oz. black peppercorns and mix with 2 oz. olive oil rub over loin and sear evenly on all sides, roast at 350° for 12 to 15 min.

224—Provencal Pork Loin

Brush the loin with clarified butter and roll in herbs d' Provance, roast at 350°

225—Bacon Wrapped Pork Loin

Saute 1 c. shitake mushrooms, cook until paste like consistency. Rub around pork loin and wrap in bacon and roast at 350° for 35 min.

226—Baked Cod Provencal

INGREDIENTS:
4 5-ounce cod fillets
1 medium onion, chopped
2 garlic cloves, finely chopped

1 28-ounce can chopped tomatoes, drained
1 tbsp capers
1/4 cup fresh basil, chopped
8 pitted black olives, halved
1 tbsp fresh lemon juice
1 tsp dried oregano
1/4 tsp ground black pepper

DIRECTIONS:
Preheat oven to 450 degrees. Place cod fillets in an 8-inch x 8-inch square baking dish. Set aside. Spray a nonstick skillet with cooking spray. Saute onion and garlic over a medium heat for about 5 minutes. Add tomatoes, capers, olives, lemon juice, oregano and pepper. Simmer for 5 minutes, stirring occasionally. Spoon sauce over cod and bake for 10 minutes. Garnish with parsley and lemon wedges

227—Miso Crusted Black Cod

Encrust cod in miso and pan sear, roast at 350° for 7 to 10 min.

228—Potato Crusted Black Cod

Brush the black cod with mayonnaise and encrust with hash browns, season heavily and pan sear to a golden brown

229—Ginger Lime Glazed Cod

Saute 1 oz. chopped ginger, add 1 tsp. cilantro, 1 c. lime juice, bring to a simmer and add 2 tbsp. cornstarch, cook until thicken. Season the cod and grill over low heat and brush on glaze every 30 sec.

230—Baked Stuffed Shrimp with Clams

Ingredients:
1 # large shrimp
¾ C. Cracker Crumbs
3 tbsp. Butter (milted)

1 C. Clams (Chopped)
2 tbsp. parsley (chopped)
1/8 tsp. Garlic powder
1/3 C. Sherry
TT Salt/Pepper

Directions:
-Pre heat oven to 350F peel and devein the shrimp, leave the pails on, butterfly the shrimp and batter in the cracker crumbs, in a small mixing bowl add the shrimp, butter, clams, parsley, garlic powder, sherry, toss all ingredients together and place on a sheet pan. Place into oven for 10 to 15 min. remove from oven and season to taste.

231—Macaroni Shrimp and Clams

Bring 2 c. manufacturing cream to a simmer and add 1 c. mozzarella, 1 c. cheddar and set a side. Add cooked macaroni, chucked clams and shrimp to a casserole dish and pour in cheese sauce. Top with 1 c. parmesan, bake at 350° for 20 min.

232—Shrimp and Clam Stir Fry

Saute shrimp and clams in olive oil and add ½ c. chicken stock, reduce by half and add 2 c. cooked rice, 1 oz. green onions, ½ c. button noise mushrooms and 3 oz. soy sauce

233—Shrimp and Clam Frittata

Season shrimp and clams, toss in 2 oz. clarified butter, 1 tsp. chopped parsley, 1 tsp. cumin. In a mixing bowl add 6 ea. Eggs and whisk smooth add the shrimp and clams, pour into casserole top with 2 oz. cheddar cheese and bake at 350° for 10 min.

254—BBQ Roasted Salmon

Ingredients:
¼ C. Pineapple Juice

2 tbsp. Lemon Juice
4 ea. 6oz. Salmon Fillet

BBQ Marinada:
2 tbsp. brown sugar
4 tbsp. chili powder
2 oz. BBQ Sauce
¾ tsp. Cumin
1 tsp. Salt
2 tsp. Pepper
2 tbsp. A1 Sauce

Directions:
-in a small container add the first 3 ingredients and refrigerate for 1 hour. In a mixing bowl add the ingredients for the marinada and mix together until smooth. Pour over the salmon fillets and place into a 350F oven for 13 min. until flaky.

255—Tomato Roasted Salmon

Place salmon in small casserole, in a separate container mix 3 c. tomato juice, 3 oz. garlic, 2 oz. pepper, 1 tbsp. cumin, 1 tsp. paprika and whisk smooth. Pour over salmon and roast at 350° for 12 min.

256—Prosciutto Wrapped Salmon

Brush the salmon with mayonnaise and wrap in prosciutto, let sit in refrigerator for 10 min. season and sear both sides to a golden brown

257—Phyllo Baked Salmon

Julienne 1 ea. Onion and place in center of phyllo dough, place salmon on top and fold close. Brush outside of pastry with clarified butter and bake at 350° for 12 min.

258—Cherry Glazed Baked Ham

Ingredients:
1 ea. Cooked Ham
1 ea. 12 oz. Can Of Cherry's
1 C. Marmalade
¼ C. Sherry Wine
¼ C. Orange Juice

Directions:
-in a mixing bowl add the cherries, sherry, marmalade and orange juice whisk until smooth and pour over the ham. Place the ham in the oven and bake at 275F for 15 to 20 min. continue to baste with the glaze.

259—Apricot-Orange Glazed Ham

Add 1 c. apricot to sauce pot and saute, add 2 c. orange juice and reduce by 1/3, puree. Pour over ham and roast

260—Red Wine Poached Ham

Bring 1 btl. Red wine and 1 qrt. Water to a simmer, add 2 ea. Bay leaf, 1 tsp. cloves, 1 tsp. cinnamon, 1 oz. black pepper corns and poach ham for 30 min.

261—Curry Ham

Reduce 2 c. manufacturing cream with 3 oz. curry by 1/3, add 1 tsp. chopped chives and pour over ham. Bake at 350º for 15 min. baste ham every 5 min.

262—Chicken Makhani

INGREDIENTS
1 tbsp. sesame oil
1 oz. roasted shallots
2 oz. minced Maui Onion
2 tbsp. butter
2 oz. lime juice

1 tbsp. ginger, minced
1 tsp. garam masala
1 tsp. chili flakes
½ oz. cumin
1 bay leaf
4 oz. sweet yogurt
1 c. manufacturing cream
1 c. tomato puree
TT Salt/Pepper
1 tbsp. peanut oil
1 # Chicken Thigh Meat
1 tsp. garam masala
1 pinch cayenne pepper
1 tbsp. cornstarch
3 oz. water

DIRECTIONS

Heat 1 tablespoon oil in a large saucepan over medium high heat. Saute onion until soft and translucent and add the roasted shallots. Stir in butter, lime juice, ginger, 1 teaspoon garam masala, flakes, cumin and bay leaf. Cook and Add tomato sauce, and cook for 2 minutes, stirring frequently. Stir in manufacturing cream and sweet yogurt. Reduce heat to low, and simmer for 10 minutes, stirring frequently. Season with salt/pepper. Remove from heat and set aside. Heat 1 tablespoon oil in a large heavy skillet over medium heat. Cook chicken until lightly browned, about 8 minutes. Reduce heat, and season with 1 teaspoon garam masala and cayenne. Stir in a few spoonfuls of sauce, and simmer until liquid has reduced, and chicken is no longer pink. Stir cooked chicken into sauce. Mix together cornstarch and water, then stir into the sauce. Cook for 12 min. over very low heat.

263—Garlic Crusted Chicken

Rub 1 oz. roasted garlic on 8 oz. chicken breast, bread in panko and sear to a golden brown

264—Potato Wrapped Chicken

Slice 1 ea. Russet potato into long slices. Carefully wrap the chicken in the sliced potatoes and brown on both sides. Bake at 350° for 15 min.

265—Chicken Saute

Dice chicken and season with 1 tbsp. cajun spice, sear over high heat and deglaze with white wine add 1 c. manufacturing cream and 1 tsp. Dijon, reduce by 1/3 and add pre cooked spaghetti pasta

266—Chicken Marengo

Ingredients:
1 ea. Onion (Chopped)
3 oz. Olive Oil
2 ½ # Chicken (Cut into Cubes)
2 C. Tomatoes (Concasse)
1 C. Chicken Stock
½ C. Sherry
1 tsp. Parsley (Minced)
1 tsp. Thyme (Minced)
1 ea. Bay leaf (Ground)
2 Clv. Garlic (Minced)
3 oz. Butter
8 oz. Chantrelle Mushroom (Sliced)
1 tsp. Lime Juice
TT Salt/Pepper

Directions:
-saute the onion in the olive oil, add chicken. Saute until brown, add the tomatoes, chicken stock, and wine. Add the parsley, thyme, salt, pepper, bay leaf, and garlic. Simmer for 1 hr. saute the mushrooms in the butter add lime juice. Remove the chicken and plate. Strain the sauce and add the mushrooms to the sauce and pour over the chicken. Can be served with pasta.

267—Chicken Monterey

Pound 3 ea. Chicken breast and season, add 4 slices of avocado and top with 1 slice of spicy jack cheese and 1 slice cheddar. Bake at 350° for 17 min.

268—Poullin Aux Fungi

Saute 2 oz. shitake, ½ oz. morel, ½ oz. oyster mushrooms. Add 1 tsp. chopped shallot and deglaze with 4 oz. Bordeaux and finish with 2 oz. butter, pour over chicken

269—Parmesan Crusted Chicken

Pound chicken breast out, season with salt and pepper. Prepare flore mixture and bread chicken. Press 1 oz. parmesan into chicken and sear to a golden brown

270—Chicken Pesto a la Lorraine

INGREDIENTS:
1/2 cup chopped sun-dried tomatoes
1 1/2 cups chicken broth
6 skinless, boneless chicken breast halves—cut into strips
2 cloves garlic, minced
1 tablespoon olive oil
2 teaspoons cornstarch
3/4 cup prepared basil pesto
1/4 cup toasted pine nuts
1/4 cup chopped fresh basil
3/4 cup crumbled feta cheese
1 (16 ounce) package fusilli pasta
2 tablespoons grated Parmesan cheese

DIRECTIONS:
Soak sun dried tomatoes in chicken broth. Cook chicken in oil with garlic in a large skillet over medium heat until done. Stir cornstarch into a couple of tablespoons of chicken broth. Stir remaining chicken broth, sun dried tomatoes, pesto, pine nuts, and basil into the skillet with the chicken. Mix cornstarch

mixture into the sauce, and cook until thickened. Add feta a few minutes before serving. Meanwhile, cook the pasta in a large pot of boiling salted water until al dente. Drain. Serve sauce over pasta, and sprinkle with Parmesan cheese

271—Tamarind Chicken

Rub 1 ea. 8 oz. chicken breast with tamarind paste and roast at 275 ° for 25 min.

272—Zucchini Battered Chicken

Blanch 2 ea. Zucchini and puree, strain and add 1 tsp. baking powder, 4 oz. cornstarch, 4 oz. flour, 2 c. soda water and whisk smooth. Batter the chicken and fry at 350°

273—Wild Rice Crusted Chicken

Prepare flore mixture substitute cook wild rice for panko and batter the chicken and pan fry

274—Dover Sole Aux Poppiet

Ingredients:
4 Ea. Dover sole Fillet
1 tsp. Pepper
1 tsp. salt
2 ea. Airloom tomatoes
1 pc. Rosemary Sprig
1 pc. Thyme Sprig
1 pc. Fennel Stalk
2 oz. olive oil
2 oz. butter
1 oz. Mozzarella
2 pc. Lemon Rounds
1 ea. Parchment paper

Directions:

-first line the parchment paper with the butter and place the lemons in the middle and the herbs after that add the airloom tomatoes then add the Dover Sole, season heavily then add the mozzarella and drizzle with the olive oil. Fold over the parchment paper and make sure it is securely closed and place into a preheated oven at 350 degrees for apprx. 10 to 15 min.

275—Sole Parmesan

Prepare flore mixture with 1 c. parmesan and encrust the sole. Pan fry to a golden brown

276—Poached Sole In Champagne

Prepare the court buillon by adding 3 c. fish stock, 1 btl. Champagne, 2 ea. Bay leaf, 1 tsp. black peppercorns, 2 ea. Star anise, 1 tsp. coriander and slowly poach the sole for 15 min.

277—Sole Florentine

Saute 2 c. spinach in brown butter with garlic and shallots. Add 1 oz. blue cheese and place over sole, bake at 350° for 7 min.

278—Estofo ConConejo

INGREDIENTS:
1—4 lb Rabbit*
4 Cloves Garlic, Finely Chopped
2 Onions, Sliced
1 Can 16 oz. Crushed Tomatoes
1 Bay Leaf
1 Sprig Tarragon
1 Sprig Thyme
2 Sticks Celery, finely chopped
1 cup White Wine
1/2 cup Water
Salt & Pepper to Taste
1 Sprig Parsley
Extra Virgin Olive Oil

DIRECTIONS:

Clean and Brown Rabbit

Cut rabbit in small pieces (approximately 18-20 pieces).

Pour enough olive oil into the bottom of large, heavy frying pan and heat on medium high. When hot enough, place rabbit in pan and brown the pieces. Remove and set aside

Cook the Sauce

Using the same pan, sauté the garlic, onion and crushed tomatoes for about 5 minutes. (If ingredients begin to stick, add more olive oil if necessary.) Add the bay leaf, tarragon, thyme and chopped celery.

Cook the Rabbit and Reduce the Sauce

Return the rabbit to the frying pan. Pour in the brandy and set alight. Add the white wine and stir. Turn the heat up to bring to a boil and reduce the liquid by a half or two-thirds. Then, add the water and stir.

Simmer

Reduce the heat, cover the pan and simmer gently until cooked–an hour and a half to two hours. (If using chicken instead of rabbit, it will take only 30-45 minutes.) While the meat is simmering, chop parsley.

Season and Serve

Season with salt and pepper. Sprinkle with chopped parsley and serve hot in bowls with fried potatoes.

279—Curry Rabbit Legs

Mix 4 oz. curry with 2 c. water and whisk smooth, place rabbit legs in marinade, let sit for 45 min. remove rabbit legs and grill slowly. Reduce marinade to a syrup and brush rabbit legs every 1 min.

280—Cornmeal Fried Rabbit

Quarter rabbit and prepare a cornmeal flore. Bread rabbit and let sit at room temperature for 10 min. and fry at 350°

281—Tuscany Rabbit

Using rabbit pieces toss in flour and sear to a golden brown in olive oil, add 1 tsp. garlic and deglaze with white wine and add 2 oz. diced tomatoes, 2 oz. sliced mushrooms, rosemary, thyme and 1 tsp. lemon juice

282—Boeuf Filet en Croûte de Sel

INGREDIENTS:
1-3/4 lb. fillet of beef
1 Tbsp. butter
1 Tbsp. peanut oil
2 ea. egg whites
1 # Sea Salt
freshly ground black pepper
Finish:
4 oz. Truffle Butter
1 ea. Thinly Sliced Truffle

DIRECTIONS:
season with the freshly ground pepper, Heat the butter and oil over high heat. When it starts to foam, add the fillet and brown it quickly on all sides. Remove it and allow it to rest in a warm place. Pour the salt into a large mixing bowl. In another, clean mixing bowl, beat the egg whites until firm. Fold the whites into the salt. Spread 1/3 of the salt/egg white mixture onto a baking sheet. Lay the fillet on top and cover completely with the remaining salt mixture. Press down on the salt to completely seal in the beef. For rare cook 20 minutes; medium about 30 minutes. For the sauce, gently melt the butter in a small saucepan. Stir in the diced truffle if using.

283—Pecan Crusted Filet

Coarsely grind 1 c. pecans and season with salt and pepper. Add 4 oz. crème fresh and encrust the filet, sear and finish in 350° oven

284—Beef Wellington

Mince 1 c. mix mushrooms and saute until paste consistency, deglaze with white wine. Cut 1 ea. 4"X4" piece of puff pastry and place mushroom duxelle in the center and fillet on top. Fold close and brush outside of pastry with egg yolks. Let sit for 10 min. and bake at 350° for 15 to 20 min.

285—Grilled Skewered Fillet

Cut 2 oz. portions of fillet and arrange on 6" skewers, season with caraway seeds, fennel seeds, salt and pepper. Grill over medium heat

286—Grilled Jerk-Style Pheasant

INGREDIENTS:
4 pheasants, skinned and quartered
1 large onion, finely diced
1/3 cup of rum
4 jalapeno peppers, seeded and finely chopped
4 cloves garlic, minced
3 tablespoons lime juice
2 tablespoons olive oil
1 teaspoon salt
1 teaspoon allspice
1/2 teaspoon thyme
1/4 teaspoon red pepper flakes
1/8 teaspoon powdered cloves

PREPARATION:
To prepare jerk seasoning, heat olive oil in a medium skillet. Add in onions, garlic, jalapenos, spices, and herbs. Saute mixture until onions are cooked. Stir in rum, lime juice, and salt. Simmer until liquid has reduced. Remove from heat and allow to cool. Rub mixture over pheasant pieces. Place in a resealable plastic bag, seal, and allow to marinate for 12-24 hours in the refrigerator. Preheat grill. Place pheasant pieces on an lighlty oiled grill grate. Cook for 10-12 minutes per side. When meat no longer appears red, remove from heat and serve.

287—Braised Pheasant

Saute 2 # miropoix and hold for later. Sear the pheasant on all sides and deglaze with red wine, add the miropoix and 6 c. chicken stock, place in 350° oven for 45 min.

288—Fried Pheasant Legs

French the pheasant legs, brush with mayonnaise and encrust in corn flakes, fry at 350°

289—Pheasant Cacciatore

Pound 8 oz. pheasant thigh. Dust in flour and pan fry, pour marinara sauce over the pheasant and top with parmesan cheese; bake at 350° for 15 min.

290—Grilled Shrimp with Smooth Mango Lime Vinaigrette

Ingredients:
¼ C. Canola Oil
1 tsp. Kosher salt
1 tsp. black pepper
½ tsp. cayenne pepper
32 ea. Shrimp

Vinaigrette:
½ C. Mango (Chopped)
¼ C. Canola oil
¼ C. Cilantro (Chopped)
1 tsp. Scallions (Chopped)
2 oz. lime juice
1 tbsp. rice vinegar
1 tsp. ginger
TT Salt/Pepper

Directions:
-in a large mixing bowl add all ingredients for the vinaigrette and whisk together, set aside. In another mixing bowl ad the rest of the ingredients and mix together. Grill the shrimp and top the with the vinaigrette.

291—Pan Fried Shrimp

Dust Shrimp in flour and pan fry in brown butter, add vinaigrette and finish with 3 oz. butter

292—Bacon Wrapped Shrimp

Season the bacon with brown sugar and black pepper, wrap the shrimp and sear for 3 min. on each side

293—Apple Cider Poach Shrimp

Make a court bouillon with 3 c. apple cider, 1 c. water, ½ c. red wine, poach shrimp at a low temperature

294—Ham Steaks broiled with Apricot and Dijon Mustard Glaze

INGREDIENTS:
1-1/2 lbs of ham steaks about 1/2-inch thick.(Can use the prepackaged ham steaks or
leftover ham)
2 Tablespoons apricot jam
1-1/2 Tablespoons brown sugar
2 Tablespoons Dijon mustard
1-2 teaspoons Tabasco sauce (more or less according to your tolerace for heat)

DIRECTIONS:
Preheat the broiler. Line a broiling pan or baking sheet with two layers of aluminum foil.
Put the jam in a microwave safe bowl and soften it slightly in the microwave. Add the sugar, mustard and Tabasco to the jam and mix well. Place the ham steaks on the prepared pan and spread the glaze evenly over each steak. Broil about 6 inches from the heat for 10 minutes. The tops should be brown and bubbly. Remove from the broiler.

295—Misubi

Cook 1 c. white rice, cool and season with rice wine. Spread rice over nori paper and place ham in the center; roll close

296—Tempura Fried Ham Steak

Prepare the tempura batter by whisking 1 tsp. baking soda, 4 oz. cornstarch, 4 0z. Flour and about 2 c. soda water. Whisk to a smooth consistency, batter the steaks and deep fry

297—Pan Fried Ham Steak In Apricot Brandy

Pan sear ham steaks over high heat, deglaze with 1 c. brandy, reduce by ¾ and add 1 c. apricot preserves; reduce by 1/3

298—Honey Braised Lamb Shoulder

Ingredients:
10 # Lamb Shoulder (de-boned)
2 C. Honey
4 oz. Red Wine
2 oz. Black Pepper Corns (Crushed)
2 oz. Fleur D'Sol
4 oz. Brown Sugar
1 oz. Cumin
1 oz. Paprika
4 oz. Garlic (crushed)
2 C. Miropoix (Diced Onion, Celery, Carrots)
5 C. Chicken Stock

Directions:
-In a heavy braising pot or Dutch oven add the miropoix, garlic, and Red wine, sauté until dark and aromatic, remove and save for later. Meanwhile season the lamb shoulder with paprika, cumin, honey, brown sugar, Fleur D'Sol, and crushed black pepper corns. Add the lamb shoulder to the braising pan and sear on all side until golden brown, add the miropoix back to the pan and add

the chicken stock, cover and place into a 350 degree oven for apprx. 45 min. check the lamb after 30 min. the lamb should be fork tender.

299—Roasted Lamb Shoulder

Sear the shoulder until you get a hard crisp sear, brush with Dijon and bake at 275° for 30 min.

300—Lamb Kabobs

Quarter 1 onion, 1 bell pepper, and cube lamb shoulder; arrange on 6" skewer. Season with 1 tsp. curry, 1 tsp. paprika, 1 tsp. cumin, 1 tsp. fennel seeds and grill on low heat

301—Coconut Roasted Lamb

Whisk 1 c. coconut milk with 1 ½ c. coconut shavings, add 1 oz. cornstarch. Rub over lamb shoulder reserve 4 oz. of mixture. Roast at 350° for 25 min. half way threw glaze with the mixture

302—Huli Huli Chicken

Ingredients:
1 # Chicken Cut into Cubes
1/3 C. Ketchup
1/3 C. Soy Sauce
½ C. Brown Sugar
3 tbsp. Sherry
1 ea. Garlic (Minced)
2 oz. Onion (Diced)
TT Salt Pepper

Directions:
-in a saute pan add the onions and saute, add the chicken and brown. Add the rest of the ingredients and cook down until light and smooth. Season to taste.

303—Huli Huli Sesame Crusted Shrimp

Toss shrimp in huli marinade and encrust in sesame seeds and pan sear

304—Huli Pineapple Chicken Kabobs

Arrange 2" cubes on pineapple on 6" skewers along with 2" cubes chicken, let sit in marinade for 1 hr. and slowly grill over low heat

305—Pan Seared Huli Scallops

Marinade scallops for 20 min. in marinade, dust in flour and pan sear in brown butter and pour in the marinade

306—Pepper Pork Medallions

Ingredients:
1 # Pork Butt
1/2 c. A.P flour
1 c. Sun Dried Cherry Tomatoes
Olive oil as needed
6 oz. Sliced Mushrooms
2 oz. Roasted Shallots
1 1/2 c chicken stock
6 oz. Port Wine
2 oz. Worcestershire sauce
2 tbsp. chopped fresh parsley
1/4 tsp. Thyme
1/4 tsp. Rosemary
TT Salt/Pepper
1/2 each sweet red, yellow and green peppers, julienned

Directions:
Pound pork medallions with your hand; lightly flour. Slice Tomatoes into thin strips. Over medium low heat, saute medallions in oil 1 1/2 minutes per side, remove from pan and Reserve. In a large saucepan, over medium heat, saute mushrooms and add roasted shallots Cook For 2 minutes. Stir in stock, Port, tomatoes, Worcestershire sauce, parsley and seasonings. Add medallions and

simmer for 7 minutes. Meanwhile, saute peppers in 2 tablespoons oil and use to garnish

307—Bacon Crusted Pork Medallions

Cook 2 # bacon seasoned with brown sugar and black pepper, add to food processor and pulse coarsely. Batter medallions in bacon and sear to a crisp

308—Sweet Potato Crusted Pork Medallions

Grate 1 ea. Sweet potato and place in mixing bowl with water. Brush clarified butter over medallions and encrust with sweet potatoes, sear and bake at 350° for 15 min.

309—Mustard Glazed Pork Medallions

Mix 2 oz. Dijon with white wine and brush over medallions, grill over low heat and continue to brush with dijon

310—Roasted Red Trout

Ingredients:
8 oz. Red Trout
2 oz. panko
1 ea. Egg
3 oz. rock shrimp
3 oz. Mushrooms
Salt
Pepper
1 tsp. Parsley
1 tsp. Chives
1 tsp. Paprika
4 oz Caul Fat
2 oz. Bacon
Sauce:
1 tsp. Shallots
½ C. White Wine
4 oz. Butter

Directions:
-Gather parsley, chives, paprika, rock shrimp, mushrooms, bacon and saute in a hot pan for 2 to 3 min. then remove let cool slightly add the panko and egg mix until evenly incorporated. Now stuff the trout and wrap in Caul Fat(Stomach Casing of a Pig) Season with salt and pepper and bake at 350 degree's for about 12 min. while that is baking in a small sauce pot add the shallots and saute then add the white wine reduce by half and finish with the butter, pour the sauce over the trout and serve.

311—Grilled Red Trout

Cut the head of the trout and butter fly; brush with mayonnaise, salt, pepper and grill over low heat.

312—Fried Red Trout

Prepare tempura batter 1 tsp. baking powder, 4 oz. flour, 4 oz. cornstarch, and 3 c. water. Batter trout and fry at 350° for 5 min.

313—Red Trout In Poppiet

Brush parchment paper with clarified butter and place sliced tomatoes and cucumbers in the center add red trout and top with fresh parsley and thyme

314—Veal NY Steak with Confit Leeks

Ingredients:

4 14 oz. Veal "NY" cut steaks
TT Salt/Pepper
1 tsp. cumin
1 tsp. Paprika
2 tbsp. Olive oil
4 oz. leeks,
2 tbsp butter
1 tsp Roasted Garlic
1 tbsp Red Peppercorns

¼ cup brandy
2 tbsp heavy cream
1 tbsp dijon mustard
¼ cup chicken stock
TT Salt/Pepper
1 tbsp butter
1 tbsp demi-glaze

Directions:
Preheat oven to 450°. Season veal steaks on one side with salt and pepper. Saute NY over low heat until golden brown. Turn and brown on other side. Place pan in pre-heated oven and cook for 6 minutes, turn and cook an additional 6 minutes. While veal is cooking: Confit leeks by cooking in brown butter and veal stock until just tender and Add garlic and saute until golden. Stir in peppercorns. Saute until aromatic. Remove pan from heat. Add brandy. Return pan to heat and simmer until reduced by half Add cream, mustard, stock, butter and demi-glaze to sauce. Reduce again Season to taste with salt and pepper.

315—Veal NY Tartar

Dice the NY finely and season with 4 oz. soy sauce, 1 oz. sesame oil, 1 tsp. molasses, 1 tsp. salt, 1 tsp. pepper, 2 tbsp. scallions and 2 tbsp. sesame seeds

316—Garlic Sous Vide NY Steak

Place NY Steak in airtight sealable bag and add 4 oz. roasted garlic, salt, pepper, and sea salt. Make sure the bag is airtight and cook in water bath for 20 min. at 350°

317—Pan Bronzed NY Steak

In a hot saute pan add the NY steak and sear heavily on one side, turn over and add 1 c. brandy, Flambé and reduce by 1/3 finish with 4 oz. butter

Dessert's

322—Coco Besitos

INGREDIENTS:
3 cups coconut flakes
1/2 cup flour
4 egg yolks
1 cup brown sugar
1/4 tablespoon butter
2 tablespoons coconut (or vanilla) extract

DIRECTIONS:
Preheat oven to 350 F. Grease a 13x9x2 cookie sheet. In a bowl, thoroughly mix all ingredients together into a dough. Divide the dough into 24 uniform balls. Place the balls on the greased cookie sheet and bake for about 35 minutes. They should be golden

323—Coconut Truffles

Add 3 oz. coco powder, 2 c. semi sweet chocolate, ½ c. manufacturing cream, melt over bain marie and whisk in master recipe, chill and reheat and chill again

324—Coco Banana Cakes

Add ½ c. pureed banana and ½ c. chopped bananas to master recipe

325—Chocolate Lavender Besitos

Remove coconut from master recipe and add 3 oz. chocolate syrup and 1 oz. lavender

326—Champagne Poached Chocolate Cream Pears

INGREDIENTS:
1 bottle champagne (750 ml)
6 sprigs lemon thyme
4 firm, ripe pears

¾ c. whipping cream
4 TBS semi-sweet chocolate powder (plus some for garnish)

DIRECTIONS:
Pour champagne into a large saucepan, cover and place over medium heat. Add lemon thyme. Peel pears and slice in half width wise. With a melon baller, remove core from both halves of pear. Place bottom halves in saucepan and cover. After 5 minutes add the tops and replace lid. Simmer for another 10 minutes. Remove pears carefully with slotted spoon and set aside to cool slightly. When cool, trim bottoms so that pears will stand up. Reduce poaching liquid for another 10 minutes. Whip whipping cream until it begins to stiffen. Add 2 TBS of chocolate powder and continue whipping, add remaining powder and whip until stiff. Spoon some of the cream onto each bottom half.

327—Cider Poached Pears

Add 1 c. apple cider and 3 c. apple juice to court bouillon and poach pears

328—Cherry Poached Pears

Puree 2 c. cherry's and whisk together with 1 c. cherry liqueur and poach pears

329—Brule Cream Pears

Roll pears in raw sugar and using a torch brule all sides

330—Cherry Lorraine

Ingredients:
1 C. Cherries
1 C. Sugar
3 oz. Milk
1 tsp. Cinnamon
2 oz. Cherry Liqueur
3 Scoop. Cherry Ice Cream
1 tsp. Mint (Minced)

Directions:
-in a sauté pan add the cherries, milk, sugar cook until almost boiling then add the cherry liqueur. Flambé then add cinnamon. Cook until flames disappear. Pour over cherry ice cream and garnish with mint.

331—Cherry Pancakes

Mix master recipes with 1 tsp. baking powder and 2 ½ c. cake flour and whip smooth

332—Cherry Cupcakes

Whip master recipe with 1 tsp. baking powder, 1 oz. molasses, 3 oz. brown sugar, 2 ½ c. cake flour and pour in S/P/S muffin pan. Bake at 350° for 20 min. top with chantilly cream

333—Cherry Granita

Puree master recipe and mix with 2 c. shaved ice and re-freeze

334—Chocolate Mousse

Ingredients:

12 oz. Chocolate, semi-sweet (melted)
5 each Egg Yolks (large)
1 each Whole Egg (large)
3 oz. Sugar, granulated
1 Tblsp. Corn Syrup, light
A/N Water
13 ¼ oz. Cream, manufacturing

Directions:

Melt chocolate over a bain marie. Whip cream to soft peaks, chill until needed. Place egg and yolk in a 5-quart bowl with a whip attachment and whip to ribbon stage. In a saucepot, cook the sugar corn syrup and water to soft ball stage,

240°F. Pour sugar into egg yolks and whip until thick. Continue whipping until the outside of the bowl feels cool to the touch. Fold in melted chocolate into the eggs, fold in cream and stir gently, Chill.

335—Thyme And Raspberry Chocolate Mousse

Add ½ c. raspberry sauce and ½ c. whole raspberries to master recipe and finish with 1 tsp. fresh thyme

336—Frozen Chocolate Soufflé

Dust a large ramekin with sugar and line the top with parchment paper. Fill with master recipe and freeze for 15 min.

337—Cinnamon-Caramel Chocolate Mousse

Mix 1 oz. cinnamon with 4 oz. caramel and slowly add to master recipe

338—Crepes A La Rayne

Ingredients:
1 Tsp. Salt
1 Tsp. Black Pepper
1 Tsp. Chervil
2 Tsp. Lemon Juice
2 ea. Onion (Minced)
1 Tsp. Nutmeg
2 Tbsp. Garlic
4 Tsp. Dijon
4 oz. Cream
10 oz. Chicken (Cooked & Ground)
4 C. White Wine
10 ea. Crepes
2 oz. Parsley

Directions:
-In a medium size mixing bowl add all ingredients except white wine, crepes, and parsley. Mix evenly and place 1oz. Of mixture into each crepe then layer

into a half 200 pan pour the wine over the crepes and bake at 350 degrees for 13 min. then top with parsley.

339—Blueberry Crepes

Add 1 oz. blueberry puree to master recipe and stuff with whole blueberries

340—Brule Crepes Lorraine

Reduce 1 c. simple syrup, 2 oz. cherry sauce, ½ c. cherries. Top with master recipe, 2 oz. raw sugar and brule until golden brown

341—Crepes Aux Benny

Remove chicken from master recipe and add duck confit and caramelized shallots

342—Lime & Basil Sorbet

Ingredients:
½ C. Sugar
½ C. water
½ C. Fresh lime Juice
12 ea. Basil Leafs (Finely Chopped)

Directions:
-in a small sauce pot add the water and sugar, bring to a boil (Simple Syrup). Remove from heat and cool. In a blender add the simple syrup, lime juice, basil and blend well. Place into a shallow pan and freeze. After frozen place into a food processor and blend, return back to the shallow pan and freeze once more.

343—Avocado Sorbet

Add 1 c. sugar, 1 c. light corn syrup, 3 ea. Peeled and mashed avocados

344—Lime Raspberry Sorbet

Add 1 c. crushed raspberries to master recipe

345—Pineapple Basil Sorbet

Add 1 oz. Thai sweet basil, ½ c. pineapple juice and ½ ea. Pineapple chunks

346—Classic French Beignets

Ingredients:

3 fl.oz. Water
¼ oz. Yeast, compressed
1 oz. Sugar, granulated
¼ tsp. Salt, kosher
2 oz. Cream, manufacturing
½ oz. Butter, unsalted
½ each Egg (large)
10 oz. Bread Flour
*** Powder Sugar

Directions:

Dissolve yeast in water. Add the sugar, cream and butter. Add the egg. Add salt, then enough bread flour to achieve a dough that can be turned out onto bench. Knead for 8 min. Cover the dough and allow dough to ferment. Punch down dough. Roll dough ¼-inch thick. Cut into 2-inch squares Fry at 350°F until golden brown. Drain on paper towels. Sift powder sugar on top.

347—3 Cheese Beignets

Toss 3 oz. cheddar cheese, 2 oz. fresh mozzarella, and 1 oz. spicy jack cheese. Add to master recipe

348—Thyme And Fennel Beignets

Roast 1 ea. Fennel and puree, mix with 1 tsp. fresh thyme and add to master recipe

349—Key Lime Beignets

Add 3 oz. fresh key lime juice and 1 tsp. lime zest to master recipe

350—Sweet Dream

Ingredients:
4 Sheets Fillo Dough
1 C. Mascarpone
4 oz. Sugar
1 oz. Vanilla Extract
3 oz. raspberry sauce
2 ea. Raspberry's
1 Sprig Mint

Garnish:
Chocolate Shavings

Directions:
-Layer the fillo dough on top of each other then fold over twice, cut into 3 in. rounds and place inside a muffin pan, bake at 350 degrees for 10 min. while that is going in a small mixing bowl make the filling by adding the mascarpone, sugar, vanilla extract, raspberry sauce and mix well. Know remove the fillo dough from the muffin pan and fill with the filling top with fresh raspberry's, mint and chocolate shavings.

351—Sweet Mascarpone Mousse Tart

Whip 4 oz. egg whites to stiff peak and fold in mascarpone. Whip 2 oz. manufacturing cream to stiff peak and fold in. Add to Master recipe

352—Chocolate Lorraine

Melt 4 oz. semi-sweet chocolate over double boiler, finish with 3 oz. butter and fold into master recipe

353—Cinnamon-Cardamom Tart

Add 1 oz. cinnamon and 1 tsp. cardamom to master recipe and garnish with shaved cinnamon stick

354—Fried Ice Cream

Ingredients:
3 C. vanilla ice cream
½ C. Granola
½ C. Powder Sugar
1 tsp. Cinnamon

Directions:
-form 3 oz. ball with the ice cream and roll into the granola. Place in the freezer for 10 min. know in set the deep fat fryer to 280F and drop the balls in, fry for apprx. 45 sec. remove and roll onto the powder sugar mix with cinnamon and serve immediately.

355—Pistachio Fried Ice Cream

Roll ice cream in crushed pistachios and flash fry at 450° for 10 sec.

356—Chocolate Coated Ice Cream

Melt 1 c. semi-sweet chocolate over double boiler and finish with 3 oz. butter, let cool to room temperature and pour over ice cream and quickly chill

357—Fried Ice Cream In Puff Pastry

Wrap the ice cream In puff pastry and freeze for 10 min. deep fry at 350° for 1 to 2 min. or until golden brown, remove and roll into cinnamon and sugar mixture

Rosario Wine Maker

Reception
Asado Parilla, Chorizo, Morcilla, chinch lines, mollejas
First Course
Formaggio Fritto Con Arugala, Prosciutto Olive Tapanada and Red Wine
Gastrique
Second Course
Homburt Cheese Stuffed Hedgehog Con Ongos Piopon
Third Course
Capello Relleno With Red Sausage Compote
Main Course
Bone In Ribeye With Jus Lie Gelee And Red Potato Anna
Dessert
Banana Frito Turnover Topped With Mascarpone Ganache

By The Sea Wine Maker

First Course
Lobster Scallopini With Saffron Velute and Matignon Vegetables
Second Course
Roasted Bison Shoulder With Champagne Poach White Asparagus
Intermezzo
Rosemary Mint Sorbet
Main Course
Honey Braised Pheasant With Fried Lily Dressing
Dessert
Espresso Triffle With Lingonberry Coulis

Astoria Wine Maker

Reception
Prosciutto Wrapped Figs and Assorted Rhone Blue Cheeses
First Course
Cold Smoked Bluenose Bass On Fennel Pommes Frits With Star Anis
Vinaigrette
Second Course
Buffalo Short Ribs With Tri-Color Raviolis In A Pinot-Coriander Glaze

Intermezzo
Pineapple Granita
Main Course
Red Peppercorn Encrusted Frog Leg Lollipops and fried Chevre Cheese
Dessert
Pomegranate Crème Anglace Ice Cream with Almond Tuille

Weber Wine Maker

Reception
Pork Tenderloin Scallopini With Fried Ginger Root Chips
First Course
Lobster Sausage In Vol Au Vent With Rock Shrimp Tomatillo Sauce
Second Course
Pancetta Wrapped Lamb Chop With Morel Cous Cous
Third Course
Rabbit Loin Stuffed With Pencil Asparagus Served With Pesto Cream Sauce
Intermezzo
Honey and Lavender Gelato
Main Course
Veal Permantier With Demi Broddo
Dessert
Tamarind Flan

Game Winemaker

First Course
Wild Boar Potsticker Fried In Soba And Pine Oil
Second Course
Ostrich Medallions On a Bed Of Apricot Risotto
Intermezzo
Asian Pear In Mint Syrup
Main Course
Elk Osso Bucco With Confit Tomatoes and Pear Sofrito
Dessert
Kiwi Lime Tart With Mint Caviar

Italian Wine Maker

Reception
Fried Octopus Tentacles and Glazed Unagi
First Course
Duxelle Encrusted Venison Loin with Pomelo Gnocchi
Second Course
New Zealand Lamb Rack Roasted In Tomato Juice
Intermezzo
Star Fruit Sorbet
Main Course
Chipolini Onion Stuffed Bear Loin With Yam Risotto
Dessert
Cinnamon Empanada Stuffed with Honeydew Paste

RECIPE INDEX

GLOSSARY

Acetic Acid—wine or cider, fermented beyond the stage of alcohol. In diluted form, it is vinegar. Also, acetic acid is used in preserving fruits to keep flesh from discoloring, and in freezing.

Achar/Achard—pickles and salt relishes used in the cooking of India

Achira—South American plant used as arrowroot

Acid Rinse—a bath of acidulated water used to prevent discoloration of peeled fruits and vegetables that brown when exposed to air

Acidulated Water—cold water with vinegar, lemon or lime juice added.

Acorn Squash—a small to medium-sized acorn-shaped winter squash with an orange-streaked dark green fluted shell (orange, yellow and creamy white varieties are also available), pale orange flesh, large seed cavity and a slightly sweet, nutty flavor.

Adobo—a Philippine national dish of braised pork, chicken, or fish. Also, a seasoned Mexican sauce made with vinegar and chilies

Agar-Agar—seaweed used as a thickening agent, as is gelatin

Aiguillettes—thin strips of meat or fish

Aïoli—A strongly flavored garlic mayonnaise from the Provence region of southern France. It's a popular accompaniment for fish, meats and vegetables.

à la—French, literally, "prepared in the style of".

à la King—an American dish of diced foods, usually chicken or turkey, in a cream sauce with pimientos, mushrooms, green peppers and sometimes sherry.

à la Mode—literally, "following the fashion". In the United States, it is food that is served with ice cream; in France it names braised meat smothered in sauce

al Dente—Italian for to the tooth; used to describe a food, usually pasta, that is cooked only until it gives a slight resistance when one bites into it; the food is neither soft nor overdone

Allspice—a member of the pimento family and native to tropical regions in the western hemisphere; has leathery leaves, white flowers and small, brown berries, has a flavor reminiscent of a mixture of cinnamon, clove, nutmeg, ginger and pepper; also known as Jamaican pepper

Amandine—a dish garnished with sautéed almonds.

Antipasto—assorted hors d'oeuvres, Italian style. Often included are ripe black olives, green stuffed olives, garlic sausage slices, salted anchovy curled on a sliced tomato, cooked dried beans in a vinaigrette dressing, prosciutto (thinly sliced fat ham) with cantaloupe.

Appetizer—a small serving of food or beverage served before or as the first course of a meal.

au Jus—French term for roasted meats, poultry or game served with their natural, unthickened juices

Bain-marie—The French term for the cooking technique we call a *water bath*

Baklava—a Middle Easter sweet rich with honey and nuts and made from filo, a paper-thin pastry in many flaky layers

Bavarian Cream—a soft, sweet egg custard mixed with gelatin and whipped cream, then flavored with fruit

Béchamel—a French leading sauce made by thickening milk with a white roux and adding seasonings; also known as a cream sauce and a white sauce

Beurre Manie—thickener made by combining 2 tablespoons butter with 2 tablespoons all-purpose flour

Bisque—a thick, creamy soup usually of shellfish, but sometimes made of pureed vegetables

Black Butter—butter, melted, clarified, and cooked until it is nut brown.

Blanch—to immerse food briefly into boiling water, then plunge into cold water. The process firms flesh, heightens and sets color and flavor and loosens skin as in tomatoes intended for peeling

Blini—Russian buckwheat pancakes served with a variety of spreads, notably, sour cream and caviar

Borscht—soup containing beets and other vegetables; it is usually made with a meat stock base

Boston lettuce—a variety of butterhead lettuce with soft, pliable pale green leaves that have a buttery texture and flavor and are larger and paler than bibb lettuce leaves

Bouillabaisse—a highly seasoned fish soup or chowder containing two or more kinds of fish.

Bouillon—clear delicately seasoned soup usually made from lean beef stock.

Bouquet Garni—a combination of herbs tied in cheese-cloth which are used to flavor stocks and stews and removed before serving

Braise—to cook meat by searing in fat, then simmering in a covered dish in small amount of moisture

Brine—a solution of salt and water used in pickling. Brine draws natural sugars and moisture from foods and forms lactic acids which protects them against spoilage. Usually the strongest brine used in food processing is a 10% solution, made by dissolving 1.5 cups of salt in 1 gallon of liquid, or 6 tablespoons of salt for each quart of liquid.

Brioche—a yeast-raised cake baked to a rich brown usually circular in shape, with a smaller round on top. It is different from other raised doughs in that eggs are added, giving it a characteristic golden tinge, also it is raised in the refrigerator overnight.

Brunoise—finely diced or shredded vegetables, usually cooked in butter or stock, and used to flavor soups and sauces

Butternut Squash—a large, elongated pear-shaped squash (Caryoka nuciferum) with a smooth yellow to butterscotch-colored shell, an orange flesh and a sweet, nutty flavor

Cacciatore—Italian for hunter and used to describe any stew-like dish flavored with onions, herbs, mushrooms, tomatoes and sometimes wine (ex. Chicken cacciatore).

Cake Flour—a low-protein wheat flour used for making cakes, pastry doughs and other tender baked goods

Canapés—Garnished bite-sized rounds of bread or vegetables (cucumber, zucchini) served with cocktails and at buffets.

Candy Thermometer—a kitchen tool used to determine heat levels in the cooking of candy, jams, and preserves.

Cane Syrup—a thick, sweet syrup; the result of an intermediate step in the sugarcane refining process when the syrup is reduced.

Cannellini—large, elongated kidney-shaped beans grown in Italy; have a creamy white color and are used in soups and salads; also known as white kidney beans

Caramelize—to cook white sugar in a skillet over medium heat, stirring constantly, until the sugar forms a golden-brown syrup

Caviar—the salted roe of sturgeon. Red caviar is the salted roe of salmon, and considered a less desirable substitute

Cèpe—a delicious mushroom.

Chasseur—game or poultry served 'hunter style', with a rich red wine sauce, or a white wine sauce, including mushrooms and shallots.

Chiffonade—finely cut vegetable strips used to garnish soups, raw, or simmered in butter. Lettuce and sorrel often are used in this manner

Chipotle—a dried, smoked jalapeño; this medium-sized chile has a dull tan to dark brown color with a wrinkled skin and a smoky, slightly sweet, relatively milk flavor with undertones of tobacco and chocolate

Chutney—from the Hindi chatni, it is a condiment made from fruit, vinegar, sugar and spices; its texture can range from smooth to chunky and its flavor from mild to hot.

Clarified Butter—butter that has been melted and chilled. The solid is then lifted away from the liquid and discarded

Compote—mixed fruit, raw or cooked, usually served in "compote" dishes.

Coq au vin—a French dish of chicken, mushrooms, onions, and bacon or salt pork cooked in red wine.

Coral—the roe of female lobsters. It turns bright red when cooked and is used in sauces

Court Bouillon—a seasoned broth made with water and meat, fish or vegetables, and seasonings.

Curing—to preserve meat, fish, or cheese with salt or by drying and or smoking.

Dashi—a clear fish stock which is the basis of Japanese dishes.

Devein—to remove the gritty, grey-black vein running down the curved top of the shelled shrimp by slitting the top of the shrimp open and pulling it out.

Duchesse—a term for potatoes pureed with milk and butter.

Duxelles—a hash of minced mushroom, shallots and herbs simmered in butter, used to flavor soups, sauces, and stuffings or to garnish.

Dredge—to coat with something, usually flour or sugar

Endive—a plant (Cichorium endivia) with curly dark green leaves and a slightly bitter flavor

Escalope—refers to a thin slice of meat or fish, without bones, gristle, or skin

Farce—stuffing

Filé—powder made of sassafras leaves used to season and thicken foods.

Fines Herbes—French, "fine herbs", usually a mixture of parsley, chives, tarragon, and chervil used to flavor omelets and in casseroles and soups

Flambe—to flame, using alcohol as the burning agent; flame causes caramelization, enhancing flavor

Florentine—food set on a bed of cooked spinach and usually covered with a cream sauce and baked. From Florence, Italy

Foie Gras—an hors d'oeuvres of seasoned livers of geese, duck, chicken, or veal made into a pâté

Frappé—a drink whipped with ice to make a thick, frosty consistency

Fumet—a concentrated stock used to give body to sauces

Galantine—a cold jellied dish of boned chicken, veal, game or fish.

Gastrique—a French term meaning to form a glaze by reduction

Gherkin—small cucumber species 1 1/2 inches long, for pickling.

Giblets—the heart, liver, gizzard and neck of fowl and small game, used to make stews, soups and specialty dishes

Gnocchi—dumplings made from a paste of flour or potatoes and egg.

Gum Arabic—a preservative made of sugar, water, and powdered acacia. It is used with leaves such as mint and rose.

Gumbo—soup or stew made with okra as a main ingredient. The term also describes the okra plant

Hoisin—a thick, reddish-brown, sweet-and-spicy sauce made from soybeans, garlic, chiles and various spices and used as a condiment and flavoring in Chinese cuisines; also known as Peking sauce.

Hollandaise—a sauce made of butter, egg, and lemon juice or vinegar.

Hominy—hulled corn with the germ removed. Hominy grits are uniform granules that are boiled and served as a breakfast cereal or as an accompaniment to a main dish or fish, meat or poultry.

Hors d'oeuvres—a light food, hot or cold, prepared for small servings, to be eaten before the main meal

Ice Bath—a mixture of ice and water used to chill a food or beverage rapidly.

Infuse—to steep herbs and other flavorings in boiling liquid

Jam—fresh whole fruit and sugar cooked into a spread that preserves well.

Jambalaya—a Creole dish of ham, shrimp, crayfish and or sausage (usually chaurice) cooked with rice, tomatoes, green peppers, onions and seasonings.

Julienne—to slice food into very thin shreds or strips.

Kebab; Kabob—minced meat or cubes of meat on a skewer, usually marinated before cooking

Kirsch—a cherry-flavored liqueur made of black cherries and their pits.

Kosher—food that conforms to Jewish dietary laws, which were laid down by Moses, according to Biblical accounts of Hebrew history

Leek—a member of the lily family (Allium porrum); has a thick, cylindrical white stalk with a slightly bulbous root end and many flat, dull dark green leaves; the tender white stalk has a flavor that is sweeter and stronger than a scallion but milder than an onion and is used in salads and as a flavoring.

Legumes—a large group of plants that have double-seamed pods, containing a single row of seeds; depending on the variety, the seeds, pod and seeds together, or the dried seeds, are eaten

Liaison—a thickening or binding agent for soups, sauces, stuffings and so on

Littleneck Clams—clams 1 1/2 inches long.

Lyonnaise, à la—"in the style of Lyons", literally, and usually featuring shredded fried onions as a garnish. Lyons is a city in central France famous for its cuisine

Madeleine—a small cake baked in a shell-shaped mold. Also, a garnish of artichoke bottoms, onions and green beans.

Madrilène—a consommé flavored with tomato, usually served cold

Maître D'Hôtel Butter—a parsley butter excellent with grilled meats or fish and vegetables, especially carrots

Marbled—a term for meat streaked with fat. When cooked, marbled meat is juicy and exceptionally tender, so this is a mark of a high-quality piece, especially sought after in steaks and beef roasts

Margarine—a butter substitute made from animal or vegetable fat and butter flavored.

Marinade—a seasoned liquid blend, usually acid-based with wine, vinegar, yogurt or lemon juice, or a dry spice rub

Marmalade—a citrus jelly that also contains unpeeled slices of citrus fruit.

Marrow—a squash. Also, the inner substance of meat bones, usually shin bones.

Meringue—a mixture of egg whites beaten with sugar and baked into cookies or used as a pie topping. The addition of sugar to a meringue is critical; poured in too quickly, the meringue will fall and will not be usable.

Meunière—French for literally, "in the style of the miller's wife", dusted with flour and sautéed in butter.

Mexican Corn Truffle—A nickname for Huitlacoche (also spelled cuitlacoche) a fungus which grows naturally on ears of corn (Ustilago maydis).

Mirepoix; Mirepois—French term for a mixture of diced carrots, onions, celery and herbs sautéed in butter. Sometimes ham or bacon is added to the mix. Mirepoix is used to season sauces, soups and stews, as well as for a bed on which to braise foods, usually meats or fish.

Mise en place—A French term referring to having all the ingredients necessary for a dish prepared and ready to combine up to the point of cooking

Mulligatawny—English version of chicken or lamb soup served with rice. The original is Indian.

Newburg—hot lobster or seafood cooked in a sherry sauce enriched with a thick cream sauce.

Nicoise, à la—dishes with black olives, tomatoes, garlic, anchovies and dried cherries. Also, a candy of caramelized sugar and browned almonds

Orzo—Italian for barley and used to describe rice-like pasta.

Ossobucco—literally, "hollow bone," this Italian specialty is made of veal marrow bones, usually shin bones, braised in wine with vegetables and seasonings.

Oven Bag—a heat-resistant nylon bag for cooking meals without basting or tending.

Oyster, Blue Point—the name for an oyster found in the waters off Long Island Sound, New York. Also, term used to refer to any good-sized oyster.

Oysters Rockefeller—oysters which are topped with chopped spinach, bacon and seasoned bread crumbs and baked

Pan-fry—to cook in an uncovered skillet in small amount of shortening.

Parfait—a French dessert of frozen pudding, either ice cream or mousse layered with fruits or syrups and whipped cream.

Pâté (French for paste)—a paste made of finely ground liver or meat blended together with herbs and spices and baked.

Paupiettes—thin slices of meat or fish, stuffed, then rolled and cooked. Sometimes the meat is pounded to thin and enlarge it, before stuffing.

Petit Four—a small cake, usually bite-sized, which has been frosted and decorated

Phyllo—pastry dough made with very thin sheets of a flour-and-water mixture; several sheets are often layered with melted butter and used in sweet or savory preparations

Polenta—Italian cornmeal pudding or mush, eaten hot or cold, usually with sauce and/or meats. It may be cooled and fried after cooking.

Profiteroles—A miniature Cream Puff filled with either a sweet or savory mixture. Savory profiteroles are usually served as appetizers.

Puff Pastry—pastry that puffs when baked.

Quahog—a hard-shell clam of excellent quality. Large size (4-5 inches), are called quahogs; smaller sizes are know as cherrystones (3 inches), and little-necks (1 1/2 inches). Quahogs are best for chowders

Quenelles—tiny mousses poached in broth, then drained and served with a savory sauce. Fish and poultry mousses are most popular

Quiche—savory custard baked in a pie shell

Ragoût—a stew made with meat, poultry, or fish, cooked simply with or without vegetables.

Ramekin—a small dish designed to both bake and serve individual portions.

Reduce—to rapidly boil or simmer a liquid until the volume is decreased through evaporation

Remoulade—a rich mayonnaise-based sauce containing anchovy paste, capers, herbs, and mustard.

Render—to melt fat away from surrounding meat.

Rennet—a substance used to coagulate milk for cheese-making, or to set certain puddings, such as junket

Roux—is a paste of butter and flour that is used to thicken almost everything in Western cooking

Sabayon—a sweet egg dessert or sauce, flavored with wine. In Italy it is called zabaione.

Saccharin—a commercial synthetic sugar substitute. It is said to be 500 times sweeter than sugar

Saffron—dried, yellow-orange stamens of the flower of crocus sativus. Saffron is available as threads and as grains. The threads are considered best, though far more expensive

Schnitzel—a thin slice of veal; a cutlet. May be breaded and sautéed, as in wiener schnitzel

Scone—a quick bread used as a tea biscuit served hot with butter and jam. British Isles

Sherbet—a frozen sweet made with fruit juice that originated in the Middle East almost before recorded history

Soufflé—a spongy hot dish, made from a sweet or savory mixture (often milk or cheese), lightened by stiffly beaten egg whites or whipped cream.

Stock—a rich extract of soluble parts of meat, fish, poultry, etc. A basis for soups or gravies

Tagiatelle—wide egg noodles.

Tahini—a paste made from crushed sesame seeds and used to flavor Middle Eastern dishes

Thimbleberry—1. A wild raspberry. 2. Any of several thimble-shaped American raspberries, especially the black raspberry

Tortellini—Italian for small twists and used to describe small, stuffed pasta shaped like a ring.

Tortilla—a round, thin, unleavened Mexican flatbread made from masa or wheat flour and baked on a griddle, eaten plain or wrapped around various fillings.

Tournedo—a small thick slice of beef fillet, considered of the choicest quality

Truffle—any of the subterranean edible fungi of the genus tuber. Prized in French cooking for its aroma, and used in luxury dishes, particularly pates of goose liver

Turnover—Pastry-dough circles or squares that are covered with a sweet or savory filling, then folded in half to create a pastry in the shape of a triangle or semicircle.

Unsweetened chocolate—chocolate liquor or mass, without added sugar or flavorings

Veal—meat from calves slaughtered when younger than 9 months (usually at 8 to 16 weeks

Vermicelli—Italian for little worms; used to describe very thin spaghetti; available in straight rods or twisted into a cluster

Vinaigrette—a cold sauce of oil and vinegar flavored with parsley, finely chopped onions, and other seasonings

Watercress—a green leafy little plant that grows only in running water, and has peppery leaves prized by epicures for salads and garnishes.

Wok—a round bowl-shaped metal cooking utensil of Chinese origin used for stir-frying and steaming (with rack inserted) of various foods.

Xoconostle—Mexican for Prickly Pear

Yarrow—an aromatic herb used in flavoring omelets, stews and salads.

Yeast—a microscopic fungus that converts its food (carbohydrates) into carbon dioxide and alcohol through a metabolic process known as fermentation

Zabaione—a rich Italian custard made by beating egg yolks until they are lemon-colored, then adding sugar and Marsala.

Zest—the thin, brightly colored, outermost skin layer of citrus fruit which contains flavorful aromatic oils and is removed with the aid of a zester, paring knife or vegetable peeler

CITED PAGE

1. Reference To Classical Dishes
Escoffier, Georges Auguste. Escoffier: The complete Guide to the art of modern cookery. New York: Wiley & Sons, Inc., 1907. **ISBN 0-471-29016-5**

Gisslen, Wayne. Professional Cooking, Fifth Edition. New York: Wiley & Son's, Inc., 2003. **ISBN 0-471-39711-3**

2. Reference To Culinary Terminology
Herbst, Sharon Tyler. Food Lovers Companion The'(Barons Cooking Guide) Barron's Educational Series, 2001. **ISBN-10: 0764112584, ISBN-13: 978-0764112584**

3. Reference To Gastronomical Terminology
L'Epicerie. http://www.lepicerie.com/catalog/category_288_FINE_FOODS_ Molecular_Gastronomy_page_1.html?gclid=COzo6tGWi5ACFQyPYAodBRQ Yrg, 2001

4. Recipes Reference
Diaz, Ben: ChefBenDiaz, http://www.chefbendiaz.com/2006, **user1261049**

5. Understanding Proteins
USDA Department of Agriculture.
http://www.usda.gov/wps/portal/usdahome,2006

6. Discovering Seafood
USDA/FDA Seafood Board
http://seafood.ucdavis.edu/consumer.html#section7,2007

About the Author

Benny Diaz started his career at the age of 5 when we would sit at the breakfast table while his father, an accomplished chef, prepares breakfast. By the age of 15 with the encouragement of his family, Chef Ben took the plunge and has not stop since, over the years he has gain knowledge from working in various kitchens under the guidance of some of the worlds greatest chefs; as a graduate of the prestigious Le Cordon Bleu Chef Ben has gain a notable reputation by Numerous reputable institutions as well as gained awards and honorary diplomas which include a Diplome De Honour from the Academie De Art Culinaire of France and Honorary inductee into the Cambridge who's Who of Culinary Professionals. Chef Ben is an abet competitor, competing against some of the worlds greatest chefs, striving to be the best Chef Ben does whatever it takes to win. As a culinary professional Chef Ben prides himself on being knowledgeable and continuing his education threw certification and culinary literature this was apparent at the 2006 chef of the year where he competed against the worlds top competitors in his category, shortly after Chef Ben decided to share his knowledge with fellow chefs threw his experience in the industry. Chef Ben began work on a culinary reference book aimed at educating fellow culinarians which is scheduled to come out in fall 2008 with all the knowledge that Chef Ben possesses he has no plans on slowing down.

978-0-595-48380-8
0-595-48380-1

Printed in the United States
118265LV00001B/270/P